Mentoring Boys To Men:

Climbing Their Own Mountains

Neal C. Lemery J.D.

to Tyler
my good friend —

Mentoring Boys To Men:

Climbing Their Own Mountains

Connect a person with
~~their~~ possibilities;
change the world.

Neal C. Lemery

Neal C. Lemery J.D.

Happy House Press
PO Box 789
Tillamook, OR 97141

Library of Congress Cataloging in Publication Data
Library of Congress Control Number: 2014918222
Happy House Press, Tillamook, Oregon

Lemery, Neal C.

Mentoring Boys to Men: Climbing Their Own Mountains/Neal C. Lemery

ISBN: 1502514028
ISBN-13: 9781502514028

Dedication

This book is dedicated to my wife, Karen Keltz, for her unwavering support and encouragement for me to express my experiences and thoughts in writing; and to the countless young men who have enriched my life beyond my wildest dreams, especially those men I am honored to call my sons: Sean, Stephen, Ryan, Daniel, and Noe.

I've changed the names of the young men I talk about. Their stories are difficult, and their lives are hard, and I respect their privacy and their courage to get on with their lives. I honor their journeys. By telling their stories, I choose to honor them and who they are becoming.

Contents

Introduction

I invite you into the world of mentoring, where lives change and souls grow. Life is best when there is a pursuit of passion and simple pleasures, surrounded by good friends, while being present in nature and relationships every day.

What has made a difference in my life is finding the passion and relationships in my life that have led me to better understand myself and the world in which I live.

In the rich milieu of my life, the real gold is found in relationships: the give-and-take between personalities, between experiences and personalities, where time and experience create a wealth of interactions and challenges. And in all that, there is growth if I choose to accept it.

As a boy, as a young man—well, and as an older man now—I have been the recipient of mentoring. As I've grown older, I've also discovered the benefits of *being* the mentor—the giver of time, listening, wisdom, and direction.

In both roles there isn't simply giving or taking but a blend of both. Often the direction of the path of wisdom and guidance isn't always obvious. The road travels in both directions.

When there is real wisdom sharing, the journey's route isn't clear. Sometimes asking the question, doing the act of questioning, and formulating the question provide the answer. Often in this journey, simply being aware of the journey provides clarity and direction. The one being mentored often provides profound wisdom to the mentor, and the process is rich for both parties.

The conversation often leads to new insights, new realizations, and new directions.

Life is never straightforward and obvious. The simple plan is only a course through the seas, and the actual traveled route is a product of the storms, currents, tides, nudges in the ship's wheel, and the occasional gusts of wind from a new direction.

"May your life be interesting" is a Chinese proverb or perhaps a curse. Robert Frost pondered the road not taken but chose to celebrate the road he did take, as it brought an interesting, challenging, and ultimately satisfying life.

The road of mentoring offers each of us its special challenges and special rewards. All too often, what I receive in the process isn't what I expected or even dreamed. Instead, I've been challenged in ways I didn't foresee, and I certainly didn't expect to live up to the demands. What I have learned—mainly about myself—has been surprising, sometimes startling, and always exciting.

Many mentors have blessed me in my life, including those people whose names and deeds of personal conversation and direction I have forgotten, at least consciously. Those mentors have given of themselves selflessly and have changed the course and texture of my life—hopefully for the better.

One of the first mentors in my life was an elderly lady whose husband had scandalously divorced her in the 1950s. She traveled the world and worked as a dorm mother in several colleges. She was a beloved friend of my parents, who welcomed her into our home on her annual visit. She'd spend extra time just with me, reading me stories and sharing little presents from the places she'd visited. Her conversations with me and around the family dinner table weren't lectures on the benefits of travel or college life, but rather they were quiet reflections, observations, and small words of encouragement to me to explore the world and dream.

Perhaps she didn't realize she was one of my mentors or even that she had much of an effect on my life, but I was ready for her words and eager to hear her stories of adventure and personal challenge. In that she succeeded, probably beyond her wildest dreams.

Each of us has been the beneficiary of mentoring in many ways and at many times. Our culture generally gives this work no name and certainly no place of honor in our rituals or tribal practices and values. The word *elder* has limited use. Initiation ceremonies and the recognition of the value of wisdom sharing are just now being slowly rediscovered. We have had to look at "primitive" cultures to see the value of mentoring and helping young people cross the threshold into adulthood with pride and honor, providing them a place from which they can fully realize their manhood and womanhood.

Yet we are truly an oral culture, a culture that honors the telling of story. Oh, we exalt in our technology and our high-speed pursuit of business and impersonal transactions. We live in small family groups and are often alone, spending our leisure time isolated and numbed by the media. Still, what we really enjoy is the telling of stories. We may not gather around the campfire or in the center of the large lodges of hunter/gatherer societies, but we still love the telling of stories, the tales of our heroes and adventurers.

Our stories, stripped of their twenty-first-century media glitz of action, sex, violence, and popularity, are still the stories our ancestors told around the fire as the elders talked with young people, teaching and imparting their wisdom and the wisdom of the ages. We all like the stories of magic and surprise, the stories that have a sweet kernel of wisdom wrapped in humor and adventure. The more passionate the storyteller, the closer we scoot toward the speaker so we can catch every word and every pearl of wisdom.

This book is a collection of experiences and lessons the art of mentoring has given to me. My hope for the reader is that your journey through these pages will stoke the fires of passion you have for making a difference in someone's life and thereby changing the course of the world. In that journey all too often the person most profoundly affected by the art of one's efforts in mentoring is you.

On this journey I suggest to you that mentoring is all around us and is an integral part of the fabric of our dynamic and challenging society.

I give you stories of young men.

They grew up without fathers or a strong, supportive family life. Their dreams were only dreams. They had no belief that they would ever realize their wants, their hopes. Sometimes they numbed their souls with drugs, their hearts empty and longing, and wondered whether they mattered.

The doors of adult life appeared to be closed to them, as they lacked the education and self-confidence to find a meaningful job or family.

These young men didn't fit into our culture's expectation of being successful teenagers. These men weren't the athletes, the scholarship recipients, or members of the "popular" high school cliques. You won't read their names in the school news or sports sections of the local paper, but you probably will read them in the police log or the court action section.

Yet they are decent young men. They are lost, and they need some help in finding their way.

They believe that no one cares about them and that they are trash. Too often that belief is affirmed, as they do not find good jobs, nor do they find their footing in the adult world.

And their lives, their experiences, have proved them right.

I live in a small, rural blue-collar town on the Oregon coast. I've watched the economy change—moving downhill, sometimes at least sideways—as the traditional jobs in logging, millwork, fishing, and farming have faded away.

Now much of the workforce serves the tourists, the second-home vacationers, and the large, impersonal corporate retailers.

Farms have been consolidated and mechanized. They need hired hands, who mainly come from poor regions of Mexico. Many people criticize the wave of immigration and support the strict new requirements for citizenship at the DMV, but only the Mexicans seem to take those jobs, with others rejecting the work as too hard with low wages. The local farm co-op now competes nationally for its marketing niche, its production base now significantly expanding in eastern Oregon, far from its humble origins as the local cheese and butter factory.

Our biggest exports are now our high school graduates. Many move to the city for real-wage jobs and college. Few college graduates return here, as job opportunities are limited to nonexistent, unless there is an opening for a professional or unless your family is willing to have someone take over the farm or the family business on Main Street.

For the last twenty years, I've been the traffic court judge. People came to me to deal with their speeding tickets, scores of other minor violations, their landlord-tenant issues, and their small claims. These are not minor court cases for them, and they want their day in court to challenge the cop, to criticize the law and the mandatory fines, and to take their lawsuit to trial. They are passionate about justice, and they look to the court and to me with hope in their eyes that there really is justice in this world.

I've listened patiently, sometimes applying the law to the facts and more often trying to explain the logic, the public policy of the legislature, and the appellate courts, the DMV. Often I was an ombudsman or a legal aid clinic staff member, referring them to resources. Many times I had been a social worker, giving some counsel and referring folks to an agency that can provide them with what they need. I tried to provide reasons why people should use common sense and principles of safety and courtesy on the highways.

I also dealt with underage drinking, tickets for small amounts ("personal use") of marijuana, and the complexities and contradictions of Oregon's medical marijuana law. And I dealt with truancy tickets and the difficulties families face as they raise teenagers. Eviction law brought me face-to-face with poverty, the tough road for single parents, and the scarcity of decent housing in the poor rural county where I live. The phone numbers for legal aid, the Salvation Army, the public health clinic, and the food bank were taped to my bench, and I often handed out my business card, which had at least one of those numbers on it.

Literacy is a hidden issue, because where I live, one in five adult males has less than a sixth-grade reading-comprehension level. No one came to court to tell me he couldn't read, and I have learned not to assume he can. When I forgot that statistic, the result of the court case ended up being unfair and unjust.

Every day I heard a sampling of what people thought about their government, the law, and the struggle of everyday life.

I'm left with a disturbing glimpse into the lives of many young men. Many of them didn't even bother to make it to court. Their frustrations and feelings of hopelessness stilled their voices as they let the system grind away, taking their driver's licenses, piling up the fines, and once again proving their belief that no one cared about them.

Yet a few did to court, and fewer still took up my invitation to speak their peace, to engage in a real conversation. When they did, what I heard was astonishing and shocking.

Their voices need to be heard, because their stories don't make the headlines, and most of us ignore them, as they live life on the fringe, not willing to stand up and be seen by most of us.

Some fade away, migrating to the cities for an obscure job or joining the swelling ranks of the urban homeless youth, living together in camps, frequenting homeless shelters, and often selling their bodies for drugs and food and a bit of love.

Some join the military, heeding the tempting arguments and offers of the military recruiters for adventure, a paycheck, health care, and the honor of being a patriot. Most importantly, they are finally able to feel that they are somebody. In my town military service engenders instant respect and honor, and soldiers are recognized as somebody, their pictures and names proudly printed in the local paper. They enlist, and most always they end up in Iraq or Afghanistan. Sadly, but not very often, they are the subject of the governor's latest order to lower the flag in front of the courthouse for a day in memoriam.

Some fall on the wrong side of the law, being repeatedly arrested but finding a home of sorts in the local jail, where they have friends, a sense of order and routine, decent food, medical attention, and at last a community that has a place for them to belong. Too often these men keep up their criminal lives, perhaps secretly wanting the routine, the security of jail—a safe place for people with little self-esteem and dead dreams.

This book is a collection of stories, experiences and lessons the art of mentoring has given to me. My hope for readers is that their journey through these pages will stoke the fires of passion they have for making a difference in someone's life and thereby changing the course of the world. On that journey, all too often the person most profoundly affected by the art of one's efforts in mentoring is you.

I suggest to you that mentoring is all around us, and it is an integral part of the fabric of our dynamic and challenging society.

Come with me into the world of these young men and be part of the change—part of making the world a better place.

one

Healing and Hope

I always wondered why somebody doesn't do
something about that. Then I realized I was somebody.
—Lily Tomlin

He cries on my shoulder, tears of sadness and loss,

No father, or a father who beat him, tells him he is nothing to him,

Emptying him of his manhood, his worth, and scarring his soul.

His heart is empty after he beat himself up again and again, telling himself that he was worthless, just like Dad said. It is a self-fulfilling prophecy, living up to his dad's hateful words.

He shakes and cries as I hug him tightly against me, giving my love to him.

I say words like *love* and *proud*, say that I am pleased by his successes. These are words he hasn't heard, but they are words his heart needs to hear.

Slowly, I see a bit of sparkle in his eyes as he starts to feel loved, my hugs feeding his soul.

There are big holes in the heart and soul of this new son.

Starved, he hugs me again, and again I give him my love, my caring for his life, my belief in his potential, his accomplishments, and his manhood.

He tells me of his dreams, his girlfriend, his baby daughter—and for the first time, I see him smile.

He sweats a bit, not sure what we are doing, but he hugs well, putting his strength into getting close to me, connecting.

I can tell he likes the idea of a dad, a man who helps him and talks about a dad's pride in this good son.

A hateful dad kicked this young man in the balls and slugged him, leaving him empty, lost, alone.

Today we sew the wounds, we bandage them, and he starts to heal.

The old dad was wrong, and now he knows it and is ready to be loved.

Finally.

These words came to me when I was thinking of the time I spent one afternoon listening to a young man dig deep into his soul, opening the scars of unhealed wounds and telling me about the dark side of his childhood. I wrote these words a couple of months later when I was trying to sort out what he'd told me and what his words had done to my soul. Now, years later, I'm up against a stone wall with this one. But it needs to be told. It's not an unusual story. A lot of men I talk to could probably tell it.

I'll call him Sam. I'm changing the story here and some of the details, some of the awful parts. The truth is too awful for me to tell. It's really Sam's story, and he's not able to tell it all. It's just too painful. I can't tell Sam's truth, and he's probably not strong enough to tell it either.

I got sick that afternoon—sick and angry—and I never felt more helpless in my life. My magic wand was nowhere to be found. Sometimes I wanted my personal laser-guided missile so I could wage war just for fifteen minutes. That wasn't the answer either, but maybe I'd feel better just the same.

He was six. His dad was gone—he'd left the family when Sam was two—and his mom lived with a boyfriend. The boyfriend was fairly new to the household, drank a lot, and did hard drugs. His mom and the guy fought a lot, and sometimes the guy would join his mom in beating either Sam or his brother or both of them together. Sometimes their crime was not doing their housework just right, or maybe they gave mom or the guy a sassy look, or maybe it was just what happened.

One day the guy called both boys into his room. Sam was six then, and his brother was seven. Sam remembers this detail because he was in the first grade and had started to read. The guy was naked, and he had the boys take off their clothes. Sam can't remember all the details, but there was sex, and it was wrong. He knew in the depth of his soul that it was wrong and evil, and it was destroying his childhood and his sense of who he was.

A whole bunch of emotions came crashing in on him, and he didn't know what to do. He was six, and he couldn't sort it all out.

Most of it got stuffed away, locked up, hidden, put away in the closet of horrors. It took getting arrested for sexual abuse, two and a half years of prison, and six years of counseling, including drug and alcohol work and about a hundred hours of our father-and-son work, to get the door opened just a crack. Finding time and trust and getting to a relatively safe place in his life started to unlock the door.

I come to visit Sam, and we find a quiet place to talk, have some privacy, and go deep. He's ready to go deep and to finally tell me what he's been dealing with all these years.

The story comes out, a little piece at a time, and not in any order. There really is a monster in this basement.

After the guy fell asleep, Sam crept out of the room and went to his mom, who was in another room in the house. He told Mom about what the guy had done.

His mom, in the kind and loving way I've seen her act with her kids, told him that the activity was normal and OK and that he needed to go back in the room and let the guy have sex with him and his brother. If he didn't, mom would beat him.

Oh, he knew it was wrong; it was evil. It was everything a parent shouldn't say or do to a child. But he had no choice. Be beaten or be abused. He was six years old, and the whole thing was out of his realm of sanity. His childhood was pretty insane anyway.

So he went back to the bedroom and the guy, and he went farther down the rabbit hole past Dante's *Inferno*.

He struggled with the guilt and shame of his sexual abuse of a young girl when he was fifteen and she was seven. He struggled with all the violence, the drugs, and the verbal hell each day had brought as he was growing up and trying to find his place in his non-childhood, his adolescent angst and turmoil, his coming of age. Manhood to him was to become the abandoning father, the abusive boyfriends of Mom, men who ran or victimized, men who drank and did drugs, and men who went to jail. This behavior was what was expected. It was his destiny.

As I listened to his ragged telling of this jumbled tale, his tears soaked through my shirt, and his gasping breath was hot on my neck. There were awful moments of silence as he searched for the hidden memories, the words to tell the story, the anger, and the rage that had festered inside his soul all these years.

There was silence—deep, thoughtful, and heavy. I gripped his shoulders and hugged him. He hugged back. Another tear soaked into my shoulder. He sobbed, catching himself, and sobbed again. We were silent, our hearts talking, his gut slowly letting loose a near lifetime of trash.

More of the story came choking out, sometimes incoherent, sometimes like a fire hose. My rational mind couldn't process it all, and I was thrown deeper into my own pit of churning pity, anger, disbelief—and yes, guilt. Guilt because I hadn't been there to help him, guilt because he hadn't gotten this all out when he was in prison and doing group therapy, guilt because he had done all that drinking and drugging to keep the lock shut tight on his closet of horrors.

Not that I could have done much. I couldn't read his mind or worm my way into his gut to find the locked-up closet door. He'd built some serious walls in his life, starting that day when his mom told him to go back in the room and be abused again. They were big walls, mortared with tears and puke and shame. That's just the way life was.

I didn't know him until he was fifteen. And a fifteen-year-old man-child isn't going to start off a relationship with an older guy, who's acting like a decent father, by throwing open the basement door and showing off the family trash. We all have our pride, and we all want to look our best. We don't like to look like fools.

None of what Sam did to get into prison makes much sense—not when you can see the whole picture, not when you finally get to the point of mucking around the closet of horrors and start taking inventory. Well, maybe it does. We are all human. We tend to behave and respond in the ways we were taught, the ways we saw other people cope.

It's just that some of us don't cope very well. I wonder how I would have coped with all that at six years old. I had enough stuff on my plate at that age, I thought. What Sam was going through was beyond my imagination, beyond my experience of what a family was all about.

"I'm sorry I'm such a f**kup," he said quietly.

Huh? I thought. *You suffering all this garbage, this abuse? You whose childhood was stolen out from under you? You are a f**kup?*

This thunderbolt jolted me out of my reverie for this poor guy, who was pouring his heart out to me, sobbing, his tears soaking through my shirt, his journey into the closet of horrors now strewing the monsters' corpses across the room.

"What?" I finally stammered, again not believing what he'd just said.

*How could he be the f**kup when the villain here was the thief in his dad's clothing, molesting and abusing this boy—the guy I'd been wanting to take out and shoot during this last hour of horror?* I thought, wanting to shout my thoughts, vent my rage, my now-impassioned lust for revenge.

"F**kup?" I whispered. "I don't understand, Son."

"Yeah. I screwed up. It's my fault. I'm such a failure," Sam sobbed, his tears falling again down his cheeks, wetting his goatee and my shirt again.

I held him close, my mind drawing a blank on how to respond. I wasn't getting this. This entire story, all this tragedy, is Sam's fault? Uh, no. Not hardly.

The silence filled the room, and I let his words just be. It seemed to be a comfortable silence, his strong shoulders still inside the safety of my arms. We breathed, and the torrent of tears subsided.

"You are such a beautiful man," I said finally.

He sighed deeply, his tension flowing out of him.

"I am?" he asked.

"Yeah. Look how far you have come. Look what you've done in your life and the things you've accomplished. You're an amazing guy."

It was quiet again. Comfortable. I could tell my words were soaking into this guy, this man-child—words he'd never heard before or hadn't let penetrate his armor.

"Thanks." He sighed, sniffling a bit, wiping his nose with the back of his hand.

I reached for a tissue, letting him clean himself up a bit, trying not to act like it was a big deal that this big hunk of a guy had just soaked my shirt with his tears and had just led me on a tour of his most secret of places, the darkest corner of his basement.

"It's not your fault, you know," I said. "You didn't have a choice. You never had a choice when you were a kid, Sam."

He looked at me, a little stunned. He nodded.

"I guess you're right," he said. "I never thought about that before. But—" He paused. "But—"

"No buts, son. You were forced. You had no choice."

It was quiet again, the wheels turning in his head. Some of the shackles and handcuffs he'd endured for most of his childhood were slipping away.

"Wow," Sam said. "You're right."

"Yeah, and you're a beautiful man."

His life got better that day, and he started moving ahead with his life a step or two at a time. That's not to say that he didn't relapse once in a while or engage in some pretty heavy sabotage of his work to improve his life.

He went back to jail again, but this time it was different. He seemed to relish the time alone away from work, away from school. He was making jail work for him: a place where he could take inventory again, a place from which he could build his life. He could see the end of his tunnel of horrors.

I went to see him in jail after the first week. During my other visits, he'd hang his head, ashamed, looking like the punk con man he seemed to think he was. Now he held his head higher, sounding confident. He had a plan, a vision. He was putting his own house in order, and he had places to go.

Every time I think of Sam's story, I shudder. The horror of what he endured that day—the six-year-old boy being abused, hearing his mom tell him he had to go back to the abuser to endure another episode of horror—and the memory of his telling are still loud in my ears.

Yet in that telling and in our hugs, there was a shift, a release. There was a lot of forgiveness going on inside him that day—forgiveness of himself. He could let the little boy go free, go find a ball and play, run wild and free, and enjoy the simple joys of simply being a kid again, maybe for the first time.

I wonder what it was like for him to put his clothes back on after that awful day and go outside and play or sit at the dinner table with Mom and the boyfriend, as if nothing had happened, nothing had changed, nothing had been lost that day.

Or what was it like when he grew into a man, when he started to date, or when he experienced the first time with a woman? The demons in the basement were there with him, clawing at his heart, howling in his ears. What lay deep inside that awful basement still came out in the night and stalked his soul, grabbing onto him and pulling him back into the pit every time he tried to climb out.

Sometimes the path to forgiveness is a long one, taking many twists and turns and taking us to places we never thought we'd have to go. Each of our paths is different, and the time we take on such a journey is truly our own. We never know when someone's kind word or offered shoulder in the darkness of our despair will be the step we need to climb out of the pit and find a foothold in our recovery.

We can offer our hand, a gentle word, and a loving embrace. Maybe a story of our own journey. We don't know what is really needed. We can only offer. But the Sams of this world? They know deep down what they need. When we offer ourselves in love with honesty and simple frankness, they will be able to take what we offer and use that gift to slake their thirst, refresh themselves, and be able to clean out their closet.

Hope can start with the striking of a match and the simple lighting of a candle in a darkened room. It can be the best gift we could ever give.

two

Answering the Call

Be the change you want to see in the world.
—*Mahatma Gandhi*

Munching on a couple of ice cream bars I'd bought at the prison commissary, we were sitting at a plastic table in the sometime visiting room/sometime half basketball court, with prison staff roving about just within earshot.

I'd been visiting Patrick for about six months now, and he'd just told me he finished writing the narratives of four men who'd sexually abused him when he was growing up. His treatment team had asked him to do that work as part of his therapy.

During one of my visits a few days ago, he'd told me about the men who molested him. Our visit had started out as just a regular visit. But he soon got serious, telling me he wanted me to know something and wanted to tell me his secret. He looked down, and I reassured him, not knowing where this was going.

"Talk to me. You've got something serious to say, and I'm here to listen to you," I said.

He cried and wrung his hands during the telling of those stories, including the predatory attack by his dad's best friend when he was nine years old. I cried, too, clenching my fists with the impotent rage I'd experienced so many times before while listening to young men tell me the stories of their lives—of the abuse, the neglect, the preying on the souls of innocent youth.

He knew I was a mandatory reporter of sexual abuse, and I would tell his treatment team. He was OK with this, knowing that I'd do my job and free him to talk about those dark times in his life, opening up to the therapists who were helping him figure out his life and nudge him to move on, to be a healthy young man. Prison was a safe place to do that tough work.

He had a lot of trust in me, and that hadn't come easily in the last six months. He'd tested me a lot. He was good at feigning stupidity and ignorance, but he was a smart young man—more streetwise than I'd ever be.

The next day after he unloaded, digging deep into his heart and letting out his story of being abused, we sat down with his treatment team, and he told his story again. His counselor and others on his support team listened—and listened hard. He poured out his heart and all that pain once again, and I could see his shoulders loosen, a sense of relief coming across his face. His pain filled the room, the air becoming close, almost choking me.

He took us down into his version of Dante's *Inferno*, telling us of horror, of terror, of unspeakable betrayal and torture, and of a childhood set on fire and turned to ashes. He became Hercules, cleaning out the sewers of his youth, setting himself free of all that pent-up misery.

At last he took a deep breath and said he was finished. He looked up, a bit of a smile on his face as he saw we were all listening and nodding our support, our compassion for his telling of his horrific tale.

"Thank you, Patrick," his therapist said. "This is a huge breakthrough for you. Now you can move forward and work on finding some peace for yourself."

Patrick nodded, letting out a big sigh of relief, a smile appearing on his face.

"I'll come back Sunday," I said as he gave me a big bear hug. "We need to celebrate what you've done today. I'm proud of you for being so courageous."

"Thanks. Thanks for being here today. I couldn't have done this without you," he said.

A few days later, we were playing cribbage and enjoying some ice cream—ice cream bars I'd bought at the canteen, which was open only on visiting days.

"I've never done this before," Patrick said.

"What do you mean?" I asked, catching a bit of the chocolate coating on my finger before it landed on the gray table the inmates had set up for visiting hours.

I was thinking the new thing was the cribbage game we are half-heartedly playing. Patrick had shuffled the cards about fifty times as he talked about his day, his schoolwork, and his work in the prison kitchen. The card shuffling was just his way of sorting out the words in his mind to give him a place for his energy as he struggled to tell his story.

Our visits always unleashed a torrent of words from him, and I no longer worried about how we would fill the two hours of my weekly visits. He had a lot of catching up to do, and I could barely get a few sentences in before he'd bury me in another ten-minute monologue of his life story.

I was the first man in his life—other than someone who worked for the prison system or the cops who'd arrested him for rape when he was seventeen—that he could talk to and talk deeply about his life and tentatively his hopes and dreams. That was new territory for him, and words that dealt with emotions and feelings were new tools for him.

He tested them out on me, wondering how I'd react to his anger, his rage, and his grief over his dad's death when he was fifteen, his mother's twisted affections and misdirected attention to him over the years, and the harsh reality of his seven-year prison sentence.

Still, prison had been a good place for Patrick. There was structure, there was safety, there was school, and people were helping him learn about what he'd buried inside himself over the years: the alcoholism, the drugs, the violence, and the sexual perversion. He could try out his new tools to express his hidden thoughts and feelings.

I was still back on the cribbage game, and I repeated my answer to Patrick.

"Is it tough to teach an old man a game you really know how to play?" I joked, my mind still trying to find out what was new to Patrick tonight. "What is the something that you've never done before?"

"Oh, no, it's not the cribbage. It's having ice cream. Eating ice cream with someone and just talking. I've never done that before."

"Oh. Really? Come on now—everyone eats ice cream. How can that be new?"

My thoughts found words, and I questioned him a bit.

"Yeah. I've really never just sat around and eaten ice cream with anyone before. Not until you," he said. "Thanks. This is really nice," he added, his shoulders relaxed, a bit of a smile on his face, a bit of chocolate stuck to his lip.

The silence filled the room, the muffled voices of the few parents and prisoners in the half basketball court dying out in my ears.

Yeah. Never had ice cream before, just sitting around and having a bit of fun.

Just shooting the breeze.

And telling his story. Telling it for the first time. Telling it to someone who cares to listen.

three

Giving Back and Glad to Do It

What lies behind us and what lies before us are tiny mat-
ters, compared to what lies within us.
—*Ralph Waldo Emerson*

"Why are you still volunteering and helping out those kids? You're retired now, and they aren't your kids. They shouldn't be your worry."

Someone asked me that the other day, his words strong and edgy
with bitterness. He wondered why I was helping others in the community, giving my time, helping others make something of their lives. It
wasn't my job, right?

I was taken aback. After all, being involved in my community is
something I've always done.

As a kid, I'd help with chores or run an errand, mow the neighbor's
lawn when he or she was gone, or feed his or her pets. I'd help out on
my grandparents' farm and get involved in some project. At dinner
there was sometimes an extra kid my mom had invited and a little more
love flying around the kitchen table. When there was a need, you just
did what was needed, no questions asked.

That idea of helping in the community has always been part of my
life. It never occurred to me to wonder why or to think that being helpful just wasn't part of living in a small town or even in the world.

Other people helped me without my asking, too. It's just what we
do. When I was a kid, a lot of people gave me the support I needed to

apply myself, set goals, and work hard. When it's my turn to be the cheerleader, that voice of encouragement, I speak up and take action.

The past two summers I've spent some time helping a young man focus on getting ready to start his junior year at a university. He's worked hard during the last few years, taking online classes and doing well, making time to study and write his papers between all the other demands of his busy life.

Now he's able to be on campus, sit in a class, and be involved in college life. He's making that transition from the technology and isolation of a computer to the excitement and interaction of a busy university campus. I've made the time to be supportive, to sit down with him and his advisors, to watch him plan his schedule, and to attend to the countless details needed to be a successful college student. It's tough doing that on your own, and when you're the first one in your family to attend college, it's also lonely and scary.

He's an important part of my family. He's lived in my village, he's part of my community, and his brains and ambition are part of the real treasure we have in our young people. He's everyone's kid. When he gets smarter, the village gets smarter, and we all benefit.

He's already a leader and a problem solver. He's got the ambition and moxie to move ahead in his life and realize his dreams. I want that energy to build our village and our country. I want to see that kind of problem solving and leadership out in the world, taking on the tough problems and thinking outside the box.

The little I do—some words of encouragement, a trip to the campus, a visit to the bookstore, a steady hand on his shoulder when the path gets a little rocky—is the best investment I can make in the future. And not just his future. His future successes, smart ideas, and focused leadership are also going to improve my life and make my village a better place to live.

I've received, and I've given back. I've come full circle in the helping-one's-neighbor view of the world. I've seen the planting and the harvest season after season. That kind of farm work—the raising up of others to achieve their dreams and reach for the stars—is what we are here for.

In the end of all that care and compassion for our fellow humankind, we might even end up with a better world for everyone.

four

Root Beer and Potato Chips

It takes courage to grow up and become who you really are.
-- E. E. Cummings

I see Steve every couple of weeks. Our time is spent playing a game and talking about his accomplishments. Tonight he's got on his best shirt and a pair of khakis.

"I dressed up for you," he says as we shake hands and sit down at the table.

He takes the games seriously: focused, attentive, a big smile showing up when he wins or when he makes a good play. He smiles when I win too, just enjoying the company and having a good time.

"I played with my dad, too," he says. "We had a good time."

I nod and talk briefly about having fun playing games when I was a kid. I make light of it, not wanting to linger. A few visits back, he talked about how his dad had abandoned his mom and the kids when he was ten, then died of a drug overdose.

Life went downhill for Steve and he found himself in long-term foster care. He was adopted. The family rejected him, and he was adopted again. That family rejected him too. He ended up in some program for lost and abandoned teens, and then he ended up here, in prison.

I make sure I show up when I say I will, and I'll play any game with him he wants to play. I buy him a coffee from the prison canteen and sometimes a cookie or a hamburger. I try to be one of the few who stick around for him, who show up and are willing to spend time with him.

I've known him well enough now that we can talk about most anything. He's growing a goatee now, and it's starting to fill in and look like a real beard. It's growing in in two colors: patches of brown and then patches of tan, almost white. His hair grows that way too.

I say something nice about the addition to his face, trying to send a compliment his way, to notice his new manliness.

"Interesting that there's two different colors," I say, suddenly realizing I might be coming off as rude or obnoxious.

"Yeah, just like my hair," he says.

"I was a failure-to-thrive baby," he adds. "I was in the hospital for my first three months, and then my mom got special formula for me. But she sold that for drugs and fed me root beer and potato chips for six months before the caseworker finally caught on. That's why my hair grows in patches, in two different colors: malnutrition."

No big deal.

He goes back to the game, studying the cards in his hand. He lays down some cards, making a brilliant play in the game, racking up a bunch of points. He laughs, telling me he's going to beat me on this hand.

Root beer and potato chips. I'm still back on that, still trying to wrap my head around a mom who would sell her baby's formula for drug money. It's no big deal. Just a fact in his life, just part of the craziness he's gone through, just his story. Another matter-of-fact anecdote to tell over a game of cards.

He's finished high school, and he's ready to graduate. He was going to go through the graduation ceremony, the one the high school has here every June, but he got sick and had to go to the hospital for three days. He missed the ceremony.

We're planning a special ceremony for him—a day just for him to get his high school diploma and a round of applause. He thinks his mom is coming in a couple of weeks—and his brother too. He wants them here for his graduation; he wants them to see him get his diploma.

She's been back in his life for only the last six months. They talk on the phone, and she's come to see him a couple of times. He says it's a good thing, and they are starting to have a real relationship.

"But when she comes to visit, I don't get any root beer or potato chips," he says, breaking into a chuckle and giving me a wink. "We're just moving ahead."

five

Why Do I Care about People in Prison?

We are all potential criminals, and those who we have put into prison are no worse, deep down, than any one of us. They have succumbed to ignorance, desire, and anger, ailments that we all suffer from but to different degrees. Our duty is to help them.
—His Holiness the 14th Dalai Lama

People wonder why I go there, to the prison in our town, and visit them. "Them": the criminals, the sex offenders. "Those perverts."

"They need to be locked up and never see the light of day ever again," someone told me the other day, scolding me for wasting my time with them.

I shook my head, stunned by this critic's hatred, his anger. Where do I begin to explain my young friends' humanity, their victimization, their desire to be well, to be productive, to be healthy? They are young men, full of love and compassion, just like everyone else. They want to get on with their lives and move ahead, just like everyone else.

When I visit these young men, hear their stories, and play games, sip coffee, and be a small part of their lives, I keep hearing the same theme time and again, young man after young man: Where were their fathers? Where are they now?

Some dads were never there for them when there was pain and loneliness and deep questions rising in their souls about life, about purpose, about love, and about finding their place in the world.

Other dads climbed into their bottles or their dope pipes, or lashed out with their fists and their angry voices, unable to turn fists and screams into hugs and quiet words of encouragement and acceptance—maybe even supporting their sons.

These dads were violent, abusive, teaching addiction and molestation, violating their sons in every imaginable way and ways I cannot begin to comprehend.

One man tells me the story of his childhood by what he has drawn and painted on a board and by showing me the scars on his body. The scars are from his dad's beatings, his mom's abuse, her prostituting him for drugs, his girlfriend cutting him while she invited him to cut on her. When he gets out of prison, he wants to cover the scars with tattoos of sacred symbols, giving himself peace and sacred honor and resolution for his angry, troubled soul.

What Father Involvement Means
- More than one-fourth of American children—seventeen million—don't live with their fathers.
- In 1996, 42 percent of female-headed households with children were poor, compared to 8 percent of families headed by married parents.
- Parents who don't live with their children but stay involved with them are more likely to pay child support. Seventy-four percent of noncustodial parents with joint custody or visitation agreements make support payments, compared to 35 percent of parents without such arrangements.
- Girls without fathers in their lives are 2.5 times more likely to get pregnant, and 53 percent are more likely to commit suicide.
- Boys without fathers in their lives are 63 percent more likely to run away, and 35 percent are more likely to use drugs.
- Boys and girls without a father's involvement are twice as likely to drop out of school, twice as likely to go to jail, and nearly four times more likely to need help for emotional or behavioral problems.

—US Dept. of Health and Human Services, *Morehouse Report,* National Center for Children in Poverty, US Census Bureau (2011)

The young men do well here, in this prison, this sanctuary from the craziness of their earlier nightmare of a world. Here they are involved in treatment and in learning about their sexuality, their anger, their humanity. They are deep in their quest for manhood. They go to school, they study, they read, they discuss, and they write. They do all that again and again. All this becomes routine—yes, normal.

They run, play ball, draw; they sing, and they lose themselves in art, recreating themselves and finding themselves as creators of beauty and peace.

They work, learning skills and the ability to earn their way in the world. They work in teams, raising and cooking their food, growing trees, restoring stream banks, improving habitat for salmon. Their work makes our community a better place, a more beautiful place. In their work they make themselves stronger, more sure of who they are and who they want to become.

They pray; they find God on many paths. They look inward and see their manliness begin to bloom. They begin to laugh; they begin to smile. They begin to move ahead, one sure step after another. They see themselves being successful, moving into the world confidently and with strength. They are becoming men—good men. They begin to see themselves in all their goodness.

At every step of their journey, they take from me, and they take from the prison staff. They want reassurance, acceptance, guidance, direction, and support. They soak it up from me every time I go there. They drain me, taking my acceptance of them, my support, my own sense of manhood.

When I smile, shake their hands, ask them how they are, play a game, or talk about their lives and my life, they soak it all up, wanting love and acceptance, wanting to be good men.

I walk away, my visit over. The click of the cyclone fence gate, with the barbed wire on top, reminds me that I'm drained of my feelings of being the son and the father and the mentor, teacher, or elder. The love and acceptance and compassion for their journey that I brought through the gate today are drained now, devoured by hungry young men needing to fill their bellies with soul food, feasting on whatever I could bring in today.

The sun shines brightly on my face, and the fresh air fills my lungs. My heart is full of purpose, of meaning in my life.

Today I could feed someone and offer him hope.

six

The Struggle Within: Which Wolf to Feed?

A Cherokee Legend

An old Cherokee was teaching his grandson about life. "A fight is going on inside me," he said to the boy. "It is a terrible fight, and it is between two wolves. One is evil. He is anger, envy, sorrow, regret, greed, arrogance, self-pity, guilt, resentment, inferiority, lies, false pride, superiority, and ego.

"The other is good. He is joy, peace, love, hope, serenity, humility, kindness, benevolence, empathy, generosity, truth, compassion, and faith. The same fight is going on inside you and inside every other person, too."

The grandson thought about his words for a minute, then asked his grandfather, "Which wolf will win?"

The old Cherokee simply replied, "The one you feed."
                                        ---Cherokee wisdom

We can often find the solutions to problems by dealing with others. Our years of life have given us some well-used and effective psychological tools and social skills to cope with relationships and survive in society. Oh, we can make mistakes and feel we are tripping over our feet, but we are actually pretty adept at moving through the social events and relationships we are faced with to get our work done.

Yet the inner work is harder and certainly darker. That work is lonely and scary. After all, we do have to face the inner problems—the doubts, the paradoxes that lie within us, festering until there is a solution or at least a resolution of some of the bigger stressors of our struggle.

We can't just walk on the other side of the street, hoping the problem will go away. It won't. It stays within us, whispering to our souls that it is still there—still here, actually—and won't go away. It is the elephant in our soul's living room.

American men, we will work our way around the issues, throwing ourselves into the eight-to-five routine, the busy schedule, or the sofa and the TV shows at night, leaving our inner conundrums on a back shelf, hoping they will be quiet long enough for us to fall asleep and avoid them for another day. Some would call this good time management.

Still, the two wolves are there inside us, hungry, growling for food and attention. Each wolf is crafty, always wanting to trick us into feeding it, paying attention to it, letting the "bad" wolf gain strength and power. The "good" wolf wants attention too, but the bad wolf is simply sneakier. On the surface, it is more fun to play with, and we give it freedom to take over our lives, driving us deeper into the shadow side of life.

The bad wolf offers us the candy and soda pop, tempting us away from the healthier carrot sticks and water or the daily exercise regimen we know makes us healthier and happier in the long run.

Mark

I came to know Mark over more than a couple of beers—oh, not that we went out drinking together. He was nineteen and got cited for underage drinking with his buddies. I'd known him a little bit because his dad and I worked out at the gym around the same time, and I'd seen Mark around town. He was a bright young man, probably destined for college. He worked hard, and he had a lot of energy.

Yet in my judge work, when dealing with him over his ticket, I could sense a lot of reluctance, a lot of anger over the ticket and the consequences. In court I was hard on him, holding him to the same level of accountability and punishment as everyone else at the party.

He didn't ask for any favors, but he had a chip on his shoulder, and he was struggling against me, the law, and the counsel of his dad. We had a good talk about his future and the real meaning of all the booze he was capable of putting away in one evening. The road signs for binge drinking and alcoholism were pretty noticeable. His dad had talked with me about it too, and he was worried.

I could tell our courthouse talk was falling on half-deaf ears, so I took another tack and wrote him a letter, hoping that the written word and the story of the two wolves would appeal to his sense of manhood and his sense of wanting to journey with his spirit and find his meaning in life. His soul was hungry for initiation and purpose, and there was a serious struggle going on inside him.

Hi, Mark

It was great to talk to you yesterday. You are headed in a good direction now, and you have solid, realistic goals.

Take time to enjoy your journey and spend some quality time with yourself, getting to know your strengths and your passions. Do some planning and write down what you want to do and what you want to strengthen and build for yourself inside. (Yeah, like a fitness routine.)

One of my rules is that I spend ten minutes a day working on a long-term goal or goals. That might be researching something I want to end up learning or making a phone call or networking with someone who knows something about a topic or skill I want to explore. In a week that's an hour, and your long-term goals are worth an hour a week.

Once a week I take myself to lunch. Just me. Maybe some paper. I have a nice visit with myself, reviewing my accomplishments, making some plans, and also taking time to say, "Good job."

I've also been learning to reduce the clutter and noise in my life. I watch a lot less TV. Instead, I pick up my guitar or my paintbrush, or I lose myself in a good book. Instead of escapist, violent movies, I pick out some interesting documentaries or really good movies on Netflix. I also spend time with my friends, and my weekly coffee with my buddies is sacred time. We connect. In a way I'm accountable for what I've been doing.

I think you will find the class very worthwhile and a good investment of your money and time. We as a society do a lousy job talking about alcohol and drugs and why we seem to be absorbed in that kind of life. Given the enormous impact of all that on each one of us, it's a worthy topic for a day.

I'm enclosing a great story—one I think will touch your heart and appeal to your spirit. (Yes, the story of two wolves!)

You are a leader. You are strong, smart, and dynamic. We need you, and we need your leadership and your voice.

So take all that energy you have from your experience the other night and channel all that into positive movement. I dare you to move on and to make a difference—with yourself and with others.

As Gandhi said, "Be the change you want to see in the world."

I double dog dare you!

Mark, I am a member of your team, and I am one of your cheerleaders. If I can be of service to you, don't hesitate to come by and grab me for coffee or lunch.

I didn't see Mark back in court for any more underage drinking tickets or marijuana—not even a speeding ticket. I'd see him around town once in a while, and he would always say hi. He settled into a job with a local company, saying he didn't think he was college material like his older brother.

But about a year later, he took the time to speak to me at the grocery store, telling me he was going to enroll in a technical college and work on some engineering classes. He was excited about that and said he was finally ready to leave town. He even thanked me for worrying about him, saying it meant a lot to him to have some adults in the town, other than his dad and his older brother, reach out and say they cared.

Mark figured out that "Two Wolves" was the story of his dilemma, his struggle. It may have taken a while, but he did figure out which wolf to feed.

Justin

This was Justin's fourth speeding ticket in a year. He'd been clocked going eighty-eight in a fifty-five zone on a windy highway through the forest on the only snippet of straightness.

"Late coming back from Salem. Had to go to work," he mumbled in court, pleading guilty.

"This has a mandatory thirty-day driving license suspension, you know," I said from the bench, using my stern judicial voice. His record had all the red flags of a lost young man, with a lot of pent-up anger misdirected into his lead foot on the road.

"Oh, how would I get to work?" he asked. He stared at the floor, not wanting to be here, not wanting to deal with all this.

I could tell he was sweating blood. We talked a bit, me slipping into my lecture about speed being the leading cause of death of young men his age and about the impact his death would have on his family and the community. What in all this would get his attention? What was the key here? I was searching through my tool bag, hoping I could connect with him.

He had the money for the fat fine—$492—in his bank account. I mentioned the fine could go up to $892. He gulped. That was out of his comfort zone. He sweated a bit more. He was making minimum wage at the jerky factory—a lot of work for not much money.

I hadn't hit a home run here, but I think I made an impact, what with talking about death and family, a lot of money, and losing his license. Maybe my work was done here.

He was the last guy in court this morning, and I could see his shoulders slump as he walked out of the courtroom with the clerk, digging out his wallet to pay the big bill for his ticket.

As I hung up my robe, I wondered if he needed something more. What more could I do here this morning? I still wasn't sure I'd reached him and gotten to the real reason he would want to zip along through the forest at eighty-eight miles per hour, dancing with the Grim Reaper.

I grabbed a copy of the Two Wolves legend. I keep a stack of them handy, ready to hand out to people I'm talking with.

I caught up with Justin as he was handing over his bank card to the court clerk, ready to pay the big bucks for his afternoon of mayhem out on the road. We talked, me probing to find out what was really going on with him. It wasn't about the money, though I could tell he hated to be spending his hard-earned cash.

He hated his work at the local jerky factory. His mom was a supervisor, so it wasn't hard to get a job there. Well, most folks can get a job there. It has the lowest pay and the toughest work schedule of any place around here. The work is grim: slicing raw meat off cow carcasses all day long and dealing with salt brines and smoking racks. There's a swing shift. It pays just a bit more. The starter jobs deal with the salt brine, with scraping the last shreds of meat off the bones and doing all the cleanup. There's lots of salt and smoky grease.

We talked about passion and anger and about living in the town we had both grown up in. We talked about dreams and hope and about being good to ourselves, treating ourselves right.

"It's not about the speeding, is it?" I finally asked.

"No."

He started to spill the beans, talking about not knowing what he wanted to do after high school, about living with his older brother, who just wanted to sit around and play video games after pulling his shift at the jerky factory. He talked about his boredom and a bit about his anger inside, about his life, about his future. About not having a future.

Using my can opener a bit, I found out he was an artist and had been thinking about art school. But, boy, that was just too scary, too unrealistic.

"Well, not really," I said. "It could be a court order."

He looked at me hard, his eyes sparkling a bit for the first time this morning in what was turning into a long conversation. That's probably not what he expected as he drove to the courthouse and climbed the stairs to traffic court.

"What do you mean?"

"This isn't about money or not driving or ratcheting up your insurance rates," I said. "It's about you. It's about your life."

I made him an offer—an offer he couldn't refuse. If he tried out art school, checked it out, enrolled, and took some classes, the fine would go away, and the license suspension wouldn't get sent to the DMV.

There was silence except for the wheels whirring in his head. His mouth sagged open, sucking in some much-needed oxygen for all the brainwork going on deep inside.

I had him hooked. It was possible. There might be an option in his life.

"Really?" he asked. "Are you serious? Can you do that?"

"Sure, if you're serious. I think you are."

He had a computer, and he could certainly find the art school's website.

"Go check them out. Set up a visit. Sit in on a class or two. Then the admissions officer will get you signed up, and they'll help you with financial aid," I said, the ball rolling in the direction I'd wanted to go with Justin all morning long. "You can do this, and you can live your passion. Do this for yourself, not for the old, cranky judge in traffic court."

He laughed. For the first time. I saw a smile and a sparkle in his eye.

He snatched his bank card from the clerk and looked me straight in the eye.

"You got yourself a deal, Your Honor," he said. "I've got to get back to work, but I'll be thinking about this the rest of the day. Wow," he said loudly to himself as he looked at his bank card, thinking of where he could go now.

He left, "Two Wolves" quickly folded and stuffed in his shirt pocket. I was sure it would be read in the car and during his lunch break at work, and it would be lying next to his computer tonight as he pored over the website of the art school.

He'd be making that call tomorrow and setting up his visit. He'd be rummaging through his stack of drawings, putting together his portfolio. He was on his way, and he wouldn't be speeding anymore. The right wolf would be getting all his attention.

We all have this dilemma of choosing the right wolf to feed. Sometimes the path that looks the easiest turns out to be the hardest. We can indulge ourselves a bit and not have to work too hard, not have to test ourselves and try the more difficult way to go.

Taking risks and pushing ourselves aren't usually very much fun, at least when we start out on the journey and realize there's a task at hand we can take on. Instead, the path with fewer rocks and bumps is right in front of us, and we can easily head that way.

We see others making that choice, and it looks comfortable, certainly acceptable. No one is going to chide us for working too hard or taking on a tough job when most everyone else is going down the other path. But we don't want to stand out and be different from everyone else, do we? Being different is harder, and there's more work in that, more risk.

We might fail. Oh, we wouldn't want that. No one wants to be a failure.

Yet we all fail. We all stumble; we all hit a brick wall once in a while. We put it in reverse or yank the wheel over, go around, and try again. We keep on plugging away and find another route, or maybe we even get another pair of hiking boots or a different truck. Maybe we even select a different goal.

Failing is actually good for us. It teaches us that one path toward our goal isn't the right one, and so we should find another path. Life has a lot of paths, and our job is to keep going until we get on the right one and not be so stubborn as to think our chosen path has to be the absolute, most certain path. We're not that smart. Life is trickier than that. Stumbling around keeps us flexible, nimble. We become better dancers.

We need to be stretched. Otherwise we won't grow, and we won't get stronger.

Being the good athlete at life, we feed the good wolf, and we take care of the strengths within us that keep us strong on our journey. We work on our nimbleness, our flexibility, and we don't get complacent in our journey. We always keep an eye out for the weather and prepare ourselves for the next storm.

We keep our dreams right up there—right on the desk or the bathroom mirror, right where we can see them. No one gets to put them away or throw a wet blanket on them or push us off the path so we are headed toward someone else's idea of our dream.

This is our life, our dream, and our journey.

Maybe Justin won't end up going to art school or moving to the big city. Maybe he'll keep his job at the jerky factory. I'm OK with that, even though I don't get a vote anyway.

But what I'm not OK with is Justin staying at his job when it isn't his dream, and it isn't his passion. He's had to give up what he really wants so that someone else is happy, or he's living someone else's dream—or even worse, someone else's idea of *his* dream.

None of us should be OK with that. That's not anyone's idea of manhood, adulthood, living with passion, or whatever it is you want to call it.

I would call it the American dream and the dream of all humanity.

seven

Wisdom from Johnny Moses

Johnny Moses is a Salish shaman and healer. He lives in Washington State but comes to our youth prison to tell stories, sing, and be a friend to all the lost men there.

In some of his stories, he shares his own story. The young men listen to this old man, a man with one lung; and they listen quietly, respectfully. His story is their story, and they become brothers.

Johnny laughs and jokes, then imparts great wisdom:

> You decide if you want to live, or if you want to die.
>
> If you decide you want to live, you also need to decide how you will live.
>
> Every day is a new start, a rebirth, a new beginning. You can't go back. You have to move ahead.
>
> Love yourself. Respect yourself. The power of loving yourself is transformative.
>
> Every adult in the village can be a parent. When you are growing up, you need a lot of parents.
>
> In the Salish language, the words for "singing" and "crying" are the same. The words for "death" and "change" are the same.
>
> Life is a process of change. Embrace that change and move on. Be reborn.
>
> In Salish culture, you are not a man until you can cry for your people. When boys learn to cry and share their emotions, then they become men.

eight

Three Men, Three Journeys

Confront the dark parts of yourself, and work to banish them with illumination and forgiveness. Your willingness to wrestle with your demons will cause your angels to sing.

-- *August Wilson*

Bill

Bill is twenty. He comes to me worried about getting his driver's license back. He owes the court money, and he starts to tell me the story of his life.

He hasn't eaten for three days, as he lost his job last week and moved out of his apartment. He can't afford the rent. He spent last night in another apartment occupied by drug users, and it was so noisy that he could get only two hours of sleep. The place was so filthy that he slept sitting up in a broken recliner.

Needing a shower, he has a three-day growth of beard and an untrimmed goatee and mustache, but he takes pride in his jeans and shirt. He has two other pairs of jeans and three shirts in his friend's car. His friend is homeless, too, and sleeps in his car. His other possessions? There are none.

Bill had a pickup, but when he was stopped for driving with a suspended license, the pickup was impounded, and he couldn't afford the tow bill or the impound fee. It's not a big loss, he says, as he only paid

$50 for the pickup in the first place. He bought it from the towing company, which impounded it and towed it back to the lot.

Bill is a logger—or used to be. His right hand got caught in a pull chain, and his middle finger has the end joint frozen at a right angle. The accident also spilled battery acid in the open wounds, and he is in constant and serious pain. He needs surgery, but that costs $4,000. His workers comp claim hasn't settled yet, and the insurance company hasn't agreed to pay for the surgery. Bill is going to the welfare office this afternoon to see whether he can get on the Oregon Health Plan (OHP). If he's successful, then he can get his surgery done, and the OHP will bill the worker's comp insurance company.

Until then, he's taking a generic Vicodin for his pain. He had to charge the prescription to his hometown pharmacy and is worried that he can't pay that bill. He doesn't want to go back to his doctor yet, as he still owes the doctor's bill.

His girlfriend is out of town, and she doesn't know he lost his job yet. They don't live together, as they don't want to be sexually active until they are married. His first wife left him after fabricating a domestic violence charge. Rather than fight it, he refused probation and mandatory counseling, and he spent a year in jail.

He had a few beers last night and is a bit hungover today after drinking on a very empty stomach. He is depressed and feels he is living up to his vindictive mother's prediction that he is worthless and deserves to fail and rot in jail.

His brother and mother shun him, and he has no place to go.

He also tells me he can't read, but he is working to take his second-grade reading level to a higher level, and he is working with a tutor at the alternative high school. He wants to learn to read, as he wants to be a mechanic, but he knows he needs to read to get his certification. So now he works as a logger when his hand works. It's dangerous work, and it may kill him, but he wants to pay his bills and take care of his kids. The court order says he can't see his kids, but he wants them to know he loves them.

His mom? Well, she has nothing but scorn for him. He never knew his dad and has never had a dad in his life. I talk to him like a dad, and I volunteer to be his dad. He starts to cry in my arms, saying he would like that very much. It's not easy for him to lose control, but in the privacy of the courtroom, when everyone else has left, he sobs quietly and accepts my hugs. I tell him he's a nice guy, and he can't bring himself to agree with me. But he nods as he cries, wanting to believe that. He tells me he wants to have a family and a home where there is love. He wants that pretty bad—so bad he aches for it.

Our conversation has moved from the courtroom, where I left the bench and my robe and sat next to Bill, listening to his story. When he says he hasn't eaten for three days, I grab my coat and walk him over to the nearby café, where I know they will make a serious effort at filling his stomach with some hot food. It is a good day for breakfast anyway. The new storm is moving in, and it is out of the north, complete with snow flurries mixed with spits of hail and sleet. The wet streets start taking on a dark sheen of ice.

Bill carefully wolfs down the breakfast I'm buying him. He doesn't want to appear too eager, but he is starving and relishes the hot food and coffee. I work at building his self-esteem, and he soaks up my praise for his character and work ethic.

If he can borrow $100, he and his buddy—the guy living in his car—can rent a room at the local fleabag hotel and not live in the car. It's $400 a month, but it will be home.

He has food stamps, and I take him over to the Salvation Army office and the local church, where the Episcopal priest is good for a voucher for food and maybe a room. It's a start, and I leave him with another hug and a brief talk about the need for him to accept some charity today. He tries to shrug off this attention, but he knows I care for him and want him to make it. I tell him I'm his friend and on his team. If he needs anything, he needs to come see me this afternoon.

The day goes by, and the late spring rain mixed with snow marks a solemn day. The workday ends, and still there is no Bill. I am hopeful that he's found a bed and made contact with his girlfriend, or maybe he and his car-living buddy have the money to rent the room.

I go home to hot soup and a full dinner in a warm house, my clean bed awaiting me and my wife greeting me at the door with a smile and a hug. My life may be Bill's dream, and as I sit at the dinner table, watching cold rain turn to snow, I wonder where Bill is tonight.

A few weeks later, Bill comes by. He is pretty excited.

"I've been thinking a lot about our conversation. I took a job—a good job—and found a place to live. I'm making some good money, and

I get to see my kids this afternoon," he gushes. "I'm paying my bills and staying out of trouble—staying away from the guys and the drugs that have led me downhill. I'm a changed man."

Bill and I talked a bit about his future during that first morning of traffic court and breakfast, and he told me he was thinking about joining the Job Corps.

"You could do the Job Corps," I advised. "You'd learn the trade you always have wanted to learn, have a place to live, get a college degree, and also save up some serious money before you graduate."

Bill said he'd give it some thought, and he did. Today, he comes to tell me he's filled out and mailed in his application for the Job Corps.

"I think I'll get in. The lady at the school thought I'd have no problems. That would just be so cool." He beamed. "It would be a great fit."

Joe

Joe is about forty and has always been down on his luck—drinking a lot, being unemployed, and having no formal education or skills. He's been in court a lot, minor traffic stuff, and he also has a few DUIs and domestic violence. His relationship ended, and he violated his ex-wife's restraining order and spent some more time in jail.

He usually comes to the courthouse looking disheveled. His hair is a tangle, and he usually has about three days' growth of beard. He always apologizes for his looks, even for being there. He is almost sorry that he's alive. Joe always comes across as the whipped puppy that has peed on the carpet. Bring on the rolled-up newspapers, and let the beatings begin.

A few weeks ago, Joe came by with a look of sheer desperation on his face. His eyes brightened when he saw me, and he told me his tale of woe.

His sister in Texas was dying. She was forty-six. She had just sent him a plane ticket so he could visit her next month. But his DMV ID card had expired last year, and the clerk at the DMV wouldn't let him renew the ID card unless he had his birth certificate. Joe couldn't get his driver's license, as he hadn't completed the alcohol counseling the court had ordered after his last DUI conviction.

So Joe had sent away to California for his birth certificate. But when he opened the envelope, he was stunned to realize that his legal name wasn't the name he'd used his entire life, and his legal name wasn't his family's name. He also realized that his parents hadn't been married when he was born. Now they were both dead. This new twist on family history was unexplained and remained a mystery. He was convinced that his dad didn't think Joe was worthy of the family name.

"What can I do?" Joe pleaded. "Is there any way I can get on that plane to see my sister?"

I told Joe about the legal process to change one's name and that it would amend the birth certificate. It was a bit complicated, as he would be asking the Oregon court to change his California birth certificate. The process would take a few months—longer than the date for his flight to Texas.

I sent Joe off to the local stationery store to get his change-of-name packet.

Before he left, I could see Joe was close to tears. I pulled him out of the hallway and into my office. I put my hands on his shoulders.

What we talked about got all mixed up in a lot of tears, a lot of guilt pouring out of his heart and shame. So much shame. I thought Joe's lifelong bottomless pit of shame would completely suck up all the sunlight coming through the window.

We did amazing work; well, Joe did amazing work. He let that filth and grime flow out of him. Finally, some of the sunlight came through and started filling him with some hope and self-love.

He set off to the legal forms store and the DMV.

In a few hours, he showed up again, a big smile on his face. He'd screwed up the courage to talk to the DMV clerk and showed him all his California paperwork and his expired license. This is a small town, and the clerk was a bit of a rebel in the world of DMV bureaucracy. There was a phone call to headquarters and a bit of saintly generosity. Joe had his new driver's license with his legal name. He was on his way to see his sister.

Vic

Vic had a bad traffic record and owed the court about $1,000 in fines. I had suspended his license and sent some accounts to the collection agency. Vic came by the other day, wanting to "make peace" and defer his payments, as he told me he was headed to jail.

"I have to serve thirty days. It's my second DUI," he said rather vacantly, without emotion.

We talked some more. Bottom line: I ended up suspending the fine on his latest ticket (improper fenders on his pickup).

"Vic, this was a fix-it ticket. If you had come by with proof that you'd put on good fenders, I'd have dismissed this. That's not like you. You're more responsible than that. You and I both know it," I said. "How come you're doing so much time on a DUI?"

"Yeah, I took the DA's deal. I kind of blew my release conditions before sentencing." Vic sighed. "I got caught by the cops in a bar drinking a week before the sentencing hearing. It was a pretty dumb move, but I was just out with my buddies, drowning my sorrows."

He didn't go to jail that night, but he did on the following Monday when the judge signed the order for the warrant.

"I think I've learned my lesson. I need to be a better dad for my four-year-old son," Vic said.

He was ready to give AA a try, but he was scared to go in this small town. Most everyone there would know him. He'd been to Narcotics Anonymous meetings a few times with his girlfriend, who was trying to cut her meth habit. He looked shocked when I said I'd go with him to AA, if he felt afraid to go.

"It's a place to get yourself together, and it's not about what others think about you when you go there. It is a place to work your Twelve Steps and work on what is important to you," I said.

He was in the process of getting divorced from his wife; and yes, booze was the primary cause of that breakup. He wouldn't lose his job by going to jail, but he was kind of at a dead end with that. He wanted to be a mechanic, and we talked a bit about becoming a journeyman and taking the college classes to get where he wanted to go.

Vic was receptive to all this, but still there was reluctance, a fear in his eyes. I wondered what that was all about. Whatever it was, it was too painful for him to speak its name.

I knew his folks; they were hardworking people. They'd raised a good son but a son whose pain in life seemed, at first, to get taken care of by the booze he drank at high school parties or while hanging out with the boys up the river. He did well in school and married a pretty young woman he'd dated in high school. He worked hard. From his drinking history on file with the courts, he drank hard too.

"It's all too scary for me. I don't think I can really make it."

I gathered he meant the booze and not the college work, and I called him on it. He winced. I had struck a nerve, and an opening appeared. I went for it.

"Don't just go through the motions on the treatment, the counseling, the probation. Find what works for you and look for the hole in your heart that you're trying to fill with the booze. What is the pain you're trying to medicate here?" I asked.

His eyes got big, and he started to cry.

"You know, I think I needed this conversation," he said. "You are right on the money. I am trying to kill off the pain. That's what I need to work on. It really is up to me, isn't it?" Vic sobbed quietly into my shoulder.

I gave him a big hug, and he held me tight, wetting my shirt with his tears and soaking his goatee with tears. The drool leaked out of his anguished mouth.

Even his work-soiled hickory shirt, with the sleeves hacked off, was getting wet. As I hugged him, I could smell his work sweat and the oil and grease from the machine shop. I could also smell his raw dread from having to deal with the courts and his freshly discussed fear of his inner turmoil and pain. That smell of pain was quickly overcoming the oily, sweaty smell of his workday.

"I can't believe you care about me. I'm just a drunk, a goddamned drunk," he cried. His big, calloused hands grabbed my shoulders, and he hugged me with all his might.

"Well, Vic, you are a good man. A bright man. You are a good father, and you have all the potential in the world to be the best man. To be a success," I said. "I care about you."

"I know you do," Vic sobbed. "I don't think I deserve it."

"Of course you do! I've known you for years, and I know you can achieve anything you want to. You just need to take it a day at a time and work on what you need to get done here. Use your jail time to do some thinking and to get the work done inside of you that needs to get done," I said.

Vic's sobbing eased off, and he grabbed my hand with all his might.

"I got more out of coming to see you today than I thought. I just thought I was coming here to defer my fines. You treated me so nice today. I can't believe it," Vic mumbled, the tears still caught in his voice.

We promised to keep in touch with each other, and he'd have time to write to me from jail.

We talked a bit about depression, and he said he probably was depressed but afraid to admit it to himself. Doing so just wasn't manly.

"Bullshit," I replied. "Depression takes many forms and has many causes. A lot of the causes are a lack of certain chemicals in the body. A good doctor can make a good assessment and diagnosis. If you are depressed, taking a good medication can often ease many of the symptoms. Drinking isn't really the best medication for that, you know."

Vic laughed. It was the first time he'd laughed during our conversation. He began to lighten up, to smile a bit through his goatee and crooked teeth. He took a breath and sighed. I finally spied a twinkle in his eyes, and he held himself erect with a new strength and resolve.

"Well, off to jail now. I need to take my son home and get him settled. Time for me to get on with the program—*my* program," Vic said as he walked down the hall. He gave me a wave and disappeared down the stairs.

I knew I'd be hearing more from him and that he'd be back to see me after his jail time. He might even take me up on my offer to take him to AA. But I suspected he'd get there under his own power. He'd made up his mind now and had another man in his life who believed in him.

nine

Compassion: It Goes Both Ways

Compassion is not religious business, it is human business, it is not luxury, it is essential for our own peace and mental stability, it is essential for human survival.
—His Holiness the 14th Dalai Lama

First, I must be compassionate to myself. Without my being fully healthy, fully aware, I cannot act in a healthy, holistic way toward others. I must practice what I intend to preach. I must be congruent with myself first and then toward others.

I am human. I am a human *being*, not a human *doing*. In my being, I am imperfect, and I can and will err. So be it. It is my nature. But in my mistakes, I learn and become more self-aware. Self-awareness leads to understanding and growing.

To grow outward requires that I also grow inward. Growing takes energy and commitment and, most of all, direction. Without direction, without purpose, there is chaos. As a human being, I am here to give direction and purpose to my life and to move ahead according to the purpose the universe instills in me and asks me to follow. I must listen to my heart and my soul, then move ahead with purpose, with direction.

A big part of this work, this mentoring and giving to others, requires self-awareness and self-care—not only the obvious but also the physical and mental. Also the spiritual. This work involves a great deal of the sharing of one's soul, one's life force.

You can get sucked dry and be left lifeless and unnourished. People who are in need, people who are hungry and thirsty, will drink and eat at your own well until your oasis starts to turn to dust.

Take some of the water, some of the soul food you share with others, and nourish yourself.

All the great prophets, thinkers, and social engineers took time off. They went to their sources, taking care of their basic needs for this work. Honor that wisdom and take time for yourself.

For me, I go to my music, to my walks down the lane or at the beach, or to a quiet evening with family, cooking dinner and sharing laughter and stories. Some minutes with my cat on my lap, with a good book, my family close, can be amazingly restorative. I make sure I spend time with my friends, and I also seek out great minds and ideas to fill my mind with new energy.

Those you mentor will also mentor you, offering some kind words, a compliment, a joke, a success story. Drink deeply of these gifts and be refreshed. You're doing good work, and it's OK to remind yourself of that simple truth.

Just for today, I will take a step forward—intentional, purposeful, and mindful of who I am and why I am here. I will listen to the directions of the universe, and I will mobilize my soul energy, moving ahead.

In all that work, I show compassion for myself and for all humankind.

ten

Being Present

Whatever you can do, or dream that you can do, begin it.
Boldness has genius, power, and magic in it.
—Goethe

It's easy to go through life not really thinking about who I am and what I'm doing at the moment with the task at hand, even with the day's list of things to get done. On a good day, it may even mean tackling some long-term project, the kind you contemplate on New Year's Day or on your birthday or at the end of a good lunch with an old friend.

If I'm in a meeting, I'm usually focused on the agenda item, trying to organize my thoughts on the subject at hand in a somewhat cohesive, intelligent manner. Then I get those few points across with some degree of skill and articulation, and then maybe I can even be a convincing conduit for my especially brilliant and insightful ideas of the hour.

If I'm having a conversation, I still find myself focusing on the next sentence out of my mouth or plotting how to wind this encounter down so I can go to the next—and more pressing—event of the day.

In those moments I all too easily pass right by the most important thing of the moment—being present, being real with the person I am with. Maybe if I really listen to that person with my full attention, my full-strength brain power, and my listening, seeing, and sensing tools, I might even figure out what he or she is trying to communicate to me.

Listening actively, being engaged, being present—all those phrases are used as a way to tell this stubborn, bullheaded guy that I need to be in the here and now for this conversation. Not off in my little dream world of figuring out my brilliant moves for the next meeting or of determining how I can balance all my day's projects so at least something gets accomplished. Or how I can finesse that song in my head or that poem that has been running around in my head for the last day, partly finished and not yet scratched out on paper.

The list of distractions goes on and on, and I find myself jarred awake once in a while. Now, where am I? What is this person right in front of me saying—*really* saying?

Yesterday I was listening to a guy tell me about how he planned to take care of a little bit of business with me. He just needed a bit more time, and he reminded me of our agreement to cut him some slack. Well, he's here, and he's asking for more time, and he's not late, so it's not a big deal with me, I thought. Sure, more time. That's fine. You checked in, and that's all that I really am requiring in all this. You're being responsible, and you are letting me know. Fine. We can be done now.

At least that's what I was thinking, what was on my agenda. My mind was on something else, something "more important."

I caught myself. *Oh, this guy's wound up pretty tight today; he seems stressed. Maybe, just maybe, this conversation is just the tip of the iceberg for this guy. He seems about ready to pop wide open. The tension in his shoulders is huge; he's even a little sweaty—an odd state for what seems like a routine business transaction.*

"How are you doing? How are things going?" I asked, actually taking the time to look into his eyes, making contact, and trying to haul up the invisible, indifferent shield I'd apparently brought to this little conversation in the hallway. My gut was telling me to pull off my business transaction face and replace it with my kind, sensitive, listening look. I do have that mode, but it often gets stuffed in the sack of "I'll get to that later once I get my business done" tumble of personas—the ones I keep stashed under my desk.

So I listened to my gut, I looked him in the eye, and I asked him a question that begged a response deeper than how he was going to pay his account.

He looked back right at me, right into my eyes. There was a spark between us, a connection. His brain threw a switch. Suddenly the dam burst. Literally burst. He gasped and choked a bit, and a flood of tears ran down his face. He gasped and sucked in a big lungful of stale office air, letting a big sigh rush out of his mouth. It got in the way of his telling me about his first child's birth this week, his imminent move to a bigger and nicer apartment, his wife's health after the birth, how his job was going, and the fact that life was pretty amazing and exciting right now, and he was really happy.

I looked at him—really *looked* at him eye to eye—and took all that in. Really took it in. All this was everything in his heart now, and the imminent explosion a moment ago had taken a backseat to this big gust of emotion and zeal. I grabbed his shoulders, which were now slowly moving down from their position of nearly touching his ears, and pulled him against me. I wrapped my arms around him, pulling him next to me so he could sob loudly on my shoulders, his tears soaking into my shirt. His chest was hard against me as he still gasped for breath.

His words fell silent for a bit, replaced by the sounds of his gasps. My hands, gripping his back, felt the tension of his muscles slowly unwind, his breaths now coming longer and more regularly.

I told him he was doing great, that he was a good dad, a hard worker, a good husband.

I thought these words would calm him down another notch and dry his tears a bit. After all, becoming a father is a really big event in a guy's life, and he seemed to have a need to have another guy celebrate that with him. He didn't offer me a cigar, so my giving him a hug and saying "attaboy" would have to do.

But all my intentions just turned on the spigot again. He sobbed even harder and gasped even deeper, and I gripped him even harder as he shook against me. I thought he was going to fall down, his legs turning to jelly and his whole body shaking and turning nearly limp in my arms.

He was beyond words, so I moved my face closer to his ear and whispered my sentence of recognition and encouragement to him again, more softly this time. He cried harder. So I just held him there, providing all the stand-up power we two men could muster together in the hallway.

After a few minutes, he sputtered out that he was sorry, that he hadn't meant to cry, hadn't meant to break down. He hadn't come here for this. Well, sure he had. He'd needed to cry; he'd needed someone to recognize that he was doing well for himself, well for his family—especially this week.

I asked him, "Has anyone ever told you you're doing well, that you are being a successful man now?"

He looked at me, dumbstruck.

Well, obviously not, I thought.

"My wife, well, she's told me, but I guess I haven't really believed her," he said.

"It's true," I replied. "You are a great man, a successful man. You have a good family, you have a baby girl, you have a good job, you are good at your job, and you are moving into a better home. You are here, taking care of business. You are being responsible."

The words kept coming at him, and he couldn't dodge them. He couldn't escape from me. I'd gotten his arms pinned down at his sides, and I had him in a bear hug, and he was crying his eyes out on my shoulder, out in the hallway in front of God and—yikes—other men. I could feel him jerk a bit, wanting to run and hide, but part of him wasn't letting go of me. His arms wrapped around me, putting me in the same kind of bear hug I'd gripped him with. He was soaking it all up, just like my shirt was soaking up his tears.

He laughed a bit, his grip easing on my back, and he was breathing normally again. The last of his tears ran down his cheeks, and he blinked hard so he could look me straight in the eye again and talk to me—heart to heart, man-to-man.

"Thanks," he said. "I guess I needed that. No guy has ever told me that before, and it's hard to believe that about me."

"Oh, but it's true, and we both know that," I said. "You are a good man."

He blushed a bit, color rising in his still-wet cheeks. He wiped the tears away with the sleeve of his work shirt, a bit of the sawdust from the mill caught in his mustache.

It was time for him to go. He didn't know what to say next, and neither did I. The tears and the hugs had said it all really. He turned to leave, needing some time to sort all this out.

"Take care, Dad," I said as he headed for the stairs. "Go home and hug your wife."

He grinned and chuckled a bit, off to kiss the mother of his new little daughter. And I turned back to where my desk was and saw the pile of projects waiting there, hoping I wouldn't find myself drifting off in thought and not living in the moment, not being fully present when the next guy came by.

eleven

The Walkabout: Finding Your Manhood

Between childhood, boyhood, adolescence and manhood (maturity) there should be
sharp lines drawn with tests, deaths, feats, rites, stories, songs, and judgments.

— *Jim Morrison*

The Aborigines in Australia have a custom that young men leave their community and go on a "walkabout." Men at other stages of life do the same thing. They leave and engage the spirit world, taking a break from daily life to dream, ponder, and open themselves to the spirits, eventually finding their role in the world and in their community.

The walkabout is more of a journey than a destination, and Western concepts of time and work have no meaning in this process.

Other cultures also have their own version of this experience, which is seen as a necessary aspect of life and of growing into manhood. It is a natural, expected, and respected part of life—sacred and intensely personal—and serves as a connection with the world and one's place in the world.

Native Americans may call it a vision quest.

However one names it, young men in our culture also instinctively want that experience. They perceive a need to leave their families, their villages, and to go out in the world and seek their purpose.

It is an intensely spiritual task—so much so that the physical destination and the rational and orderly aspects of a search for a job, education, or even adventure are secondary.

Sadly, our culture doesn't even have words for this, and we don't celebrate our youth as they are called to the journey, nor do we welcome and honor their return or the spiritual changes they have experienced during the process.

When men don't have this experience, they remain hungry, empty inside—lacking that sense of accomplishment and self-exploration and connection with Spirit that meets their needs to grow into manhood, to make peace with the conflicts in their struggle, and to fully understand and take on the mantle of their masculinity.

Instead our culture has a backhanded, not quite honored, place for this in the act of getting a driver's license, joining the military, losing one's virginity, or experimenting with alcohol or drugs. These activities, these empty rituals, are often done privately, with no celebration by the village, no celebration on his return, and no honoring of a young man's innate desire to confront and join in his spiritual quest for manhood or to explore his self and celebrate his soul.

There is no crowd in the village square cheering on his accomplishments.

Chris

One of my sons desperately hungered for such an experience. He left us before he could come into his own and remained lost. He is the prodigal son who has yet to return.

I mailed this letter to a person who still had contact with him, asking him or her to give it to him. I haven't heard back, but I like to think my son got my letter.

> Dear Chris,
>
> I haven't heard from you for too long. I hope you are well and that you are doing the emotional work that you need to do.
>
> I wait. I wait to have a meaningful conversation with my son. I wait for that conversation, because I know it will happen sometime, and the conversation will be

honest and open, and it will occur with love from both of us. In that conversation will be the spirit of forgiveness.

I wait. I wait to build a relationship with my son. The relationship must be based on honesty and mutual respect, for those are the values that I, as a father, must share with my son. It is my duty as a father to challenge my son to live his life honestly and respectfully and with love—both love of self and love of others. I expect my son to hold me to those same values.

I wait. I wait for my son to find happiness and a purpose in life. I wait for that happiness and purpose to be based on love of himself and love of God and respect for self and others. I know that will happen over time.

I must be patient, for this work is hard. But I also know that this work can be done. When my son is ready, this work will be done.

I suggest to you that this work, while hard and soul-searching and tough, is still easier than the work of living away from truth and love and honesty and self-respect. Dope and booze and deception are only garbage, only roadblocks. Those things keep you from God and keep you from Chris. I suggest that it is time to clean house and chase the rats out. Your foundation is firm and strong. Build a new house—strong, secure, and free of trash.

I do not write this to degrade or belittle or condemn my son. I do not write these words in anger or rage, or to be abusive or condemning. To do that serves no purpose and prevents my son from traveling on his journey. Instead, I write to speak my heart and to communicate my love and my expectations for my son. It is my duty to God and my son not to condemn or belittle or to speak in rage or with malice.

In the past, I have looked into the heart and soul of my son, and I have found deep down that honesty and respect and love. I know he is a child of God and that he is deep down a person of those morals and values. I pray that he realizes this and then builds a life on those foundations.

Chris, what have you found inside yourself deep down? Do you see the same values I see deep down? They are there. They live in your heart. I want you to let them fill your heart.

When you were fifteen and we went on our hiking and rafting trip, and when you were getting ready for court, you and I spoke our hearts to each other, and I looked into your heart and soul. Our conversations around the campfire and as we watched the sunrise over the lake were full of truth and openness. I saw purity and goodness and decency. If there is garbage in the way of your viewing those values and your heart and your soul, it is time to remove the garbage, dig deep, and rediscover those values you have inside you.

It's up to you. I know you can do this. A fresh start opens up a healthy and new path. Each journey begins with one step.

Not doing this now—and being silent about the discussions and work that need to happen—is to simply prolong and intensify the pain.

I wait. I will be patient.

When you are ready for an honest conversation, I will come. I wait.

Love,
Neal

When the father, the mentor, knows that the young man is hungering for the journey—the walkabout—there is a challenge.

I've wanted to grab my magic wand and make it all well. I've wanted to lead the son on the walkabout and to be part of that journey. Yet the father must stay in the village and wait for the son to be off on his own walkabout.

This is not the story of the father's walkabout. This is a journey only the son can take. The father must stay at home and be on that journey only by being carried within the son's heart. Having the father's support for the journey is important, but it is for the son to take the journey—to take the first step and start out on his own.

For many sons there is the terror of stepping outside the house, leaving the village with little to carry in the knapsack, undertaking the journey into the spirit world, and wrestling with the demons that have plagued the son's life—demons that have kept him from fully realizing his manhood. The world can be dark and filled with enemies.

Once the son becomes a man, there comes responsibility and duty and all that comes with being a man. Childhood is to be left behind, and one now has to be responsible. It is a daunting undertaking.

One might make a mistake and fail. One might look foolish and be embarrassed.

Boyhood, from that perspective, looks safe and inviting and comforting. Yet part of the young man yearns for manhood for its promised independence and prestige and power. The young man is pulled in both directions.

The good mentor understands all this and has the wisdom of waiting and providing quiet reassurance and guidance. Above all, the mentor provides an example of the healthy, self-confident, self-aware man who is comfortable in his own manly loincloth and holds his own spear and shield with strength and a sense of experienced ease.

The mentor has also had the benefit of his own walkabout, and the inner glow, the spiritual blessings, of that experience radiate from his being to such an extent that the young man readily sees the relaxed acceptance of the mentor of this cloak of masculinity and the natural acceptance of the role of being a man.

The mentor carries this strength without the need for violence, drinking, yelling, "ruling the roost," and all the other phony personas men display when they are insecure in their own masculinity and don't have the confidence in themselves to fully be men.

Growing into manhood is a daunting task. Our culture pulls us away from this role, this acceptance and comfort. We are supposed to self-medicate, we are supposed to be weak, and we are supposed to thrive on turmoil and gossip and sensationalism. We are supposed to be crude and unloving and dependent on the media and commercialism for our true values and beliefs. We are macho studs, aren't we?

True mentoring is done quietly, respectfully, with a sense of the spiritual nourishment and blessings that quiet conversation and respect for youth and the search for knowledge can offer. It is not a time for multitasking or for a few nudges and winks during the televised football game while sharing a beer.

It is speaking from the heart and letting one's soul shine bright and solidly, with purpose, love, and spirit.

It is true mentoring—true parenting.

twelve

Redoing the Landscape

One generation plants the trees, the next gets the shade.
—*Chinese proverb*

Peter

I met Peter when he came to court for a marijuana ticket. He pleaded guilty; he'd had a joint in the car his buddy was driving. They got stopped on a narrow, twisty road in the forest for speeding, and the joint in his car was fresh. The joint filled the car, and the trooper's nose, with the strong odor of pot.

He didn't qualify for diversion, as he'd had a DUI a couple of years ago. He'd gone to a party, not feeling like he fit in, and gotten drunk; then, stupidly, he'd tried to drive home and got caught.

He showed up in court all alone, dressed neatly in jeans and a nice plaid long-sleeved shirt. He was a little scruffy, with a couple of days of stubble on his face; and his hair was tousled, as if he hadn't combed it before driving over here from the city.

We talked about the penalties, including the license suspension. He started to sob, and I ended up taking off my robe and sitting down next to him, bringing a box of tissues. Big tears rolled down his stubbled cheeks as he told me about his life.

He'd worked at a large garden store and nursery, but he was laid off in the fall. When he went back recently to see if he could work there again this year, one of the bosses put him down, mocking him, and asked him whether he'd decided to grow up yet.

Peter was twenty-eight, and his girlfriend for the last few years had moved in with him last year. They were planning a big wedding in a year and a half at the beach. She was a technician for a veterinarian and had a good, stable job with benefits. But they weren't married, so he didn't have health or dental insurance.

He got unemployment and worked a few part-time odd jobs, but mainly he sat around the apartment, watching TV, applying for work online, and getting more depressed.

He referred to himself as a "jackass" and "immature." He said he needed to "grow up." He saw himself as a sort of mascot at parties and social events, and he kept to himself. He had no close friends, but he saw his girlfriend and his mom as people he could have a serious talk with. His male buddies were the drinkers and pot smokers he wished he didn't hang out with, as he saw himself as not being the drinker or pot smoker anymore.

He'd had some community college classes in welding and had a certificate in welding, but he also loved landscaping work and would like to keep working in the nursery or landscaping business.

Peter didn't smile, as he believed his teeth were ugly and crooked. When I talked with him about getting married now so he could get medical and dental care, he seemed surprised. He'd never considered getting married to be able to get his teeth straightened.

I asked him about why he'd come to court unshaven and looking unkempt. He said he was trying to grow a beard. But he felt he was a failure at being able to grow a beard, as it itched after a day or two. He couldn't do anything right. We talked about growing beards, and I found out he washed his face and his stubble with soap. I told him about washing with shampoo and using lots of conditioner the first week, and he seemed intent now on growing a beard or at least a mustache and a goatee.

Peter was depressed; he didn't exercise or get out except to turn in job applications. He kept crying during our conversation, and he filled five tissues with his tears, sobbing hard at times as he poured out his life story.

He had no father and a lot of anger about that and toward the father who had abandoned him at what I suspected was a very early age for Peter. The dad had never been around for Peter. His body would shake with anger and rage when I asked about his dad.

Peter sometimes went to church and talked to God but only when he needed something, and he pleaded with God for help. He had no real relationship with his minister or with other guys in the church, and he saw his religious life as a place to be the sinner and failure he was.

As we ended our discussion, I gave Peter a job. He had to come up with a plan for his life, a "landscaping plan" that would include some volunteer work, some schooling, or at least investigating some landscaping classes at his community college, which was a few miles from his house. He needed to develop a good social life and "weed out" the "friends" who were bad influences in his life.

He finally let me hug him as he left. He dried his tears and gave me several big hugs and handshakes. He has my e-mail address, and I hope to hear from him next week with his "landscaping plan."

I also told him to stop by the river on his way home and find some rocks. He needed to physically throw away those toxic people and poisonous ideas. He would then see the names of people and the issues he was angry about. In that physical act, his rage would be released, and he could move on. He liked that idea and was thinking about that list when he left.

Well, about six months later, Peter came by. I didn't recognize him. He was neat and clean, and he proudly showed me his neatly trimmed mustache and goatee. He'd gotten through two terms of welding classes, and he proudly showed me his certificate. He was taking a few more classes there, as he was interested in doing some drafting and learning AutoCAD.

His relationship with his girlfriend had blossomed, and he was just one big happy smile. He'd started his own landscaping business on the side and worked his hours around his classes. He was making money, he had a lot of referrals from his customers, and a lot of the customers at the nursery had become his clients.

Marijuana was a thing of the past for him, though some of his friends still smoked. He'd realized it was getting in the way of his relationship with his girlfriend, and it wasn't doing any good for his health and his depression.

He shook my hand and gave me another hug.

As we go through life, we sometimes need to get out the pruning shears, cut out the deadwood, and reenergize the root stock by taking out some of the unnecessary limbs and branches. When we prune, we let in more fresh air and sunlight, and the plant grows healthier and stronger.

Pruning is a good thing, and we all need to tend to our gardens.

thirteen

Being in Solitude

The events in our lives happen in a sequence in time, but in their significance to ourselves, they find their own order...the continuous thread of revelation."
—Eudora Welty

The first summer my foster sons were with us, I decided to take a week off and spend some time with them—real time—getting to know them and offering them an experience of family life and fathering. I'd always gone camping or hiking during the summer. It had been part of my family life since before I was born, and our home movies have a clip of me toddling by a mountain lake when I was in diapers. It was just what we did.

My interest in taking my sons camping redoubled when I found out they had never gone on an overnight hike, and they hadn't experienced being in the Cascade Mountains, the major mountain range of the Northwest. They'd lived in Oregon for about five years, but they didn't know their home state.

Boys not knowing about camping and mountains? Boys who hadn't gone fishing in a mountain lake? Boys not sitting around a campfire? Not swimming in a lake? Oh, this wouldn't do. They needed the experience, especially if they were members of this family.

They were pretty interested in the preparation, and I'd borrowed a few backpacks from a friend. I packed enough food for a small army, even though we were going to be out on the trail for only four days. I rounded up our fishing gear, and we headed off. I stopped off at a store to get a better camera, not wanting to miss capturing this adventure with these young men.

That afternoon we arrived at the trailhead, and I could tell the younger boy was a little anxious as I locked the car and shouldered my pack. He fell silent and followed me up the trail. Soon we were climbing among some big trees, and the big North Woods got darker and deeper. We were leaving his familiar world.

The older boy leaped up the trail, sensing this was adventure and that he would be the first to get to the lake, which was four miles away. He had enough energy that he'd come back once in a while to assess our progress and report on where the trail went.

I had to stop once in a while to regain my breath, feeling the weight of the tent, the hiker's stove, and all the food I'd stashed away. The younger boy's face was lined with worry, and he admitted he was scared.

We talked a bit about having an adventure and about the fact that a lot of people had used this trail and that there were plenty of nice places to camp by the lake.

"What are we going to do there?" he asked, his voice shaking a bit.

"Just relax, enjoy the scenery, fish a bit. Whatever you want," I said, trying to calm his fears.

This was the same boy who, when I took them to the beach the first weekend they were with us and brought the family dog, stood by the car and stared at the beach, muttering that he didn't know what we were doing there. I had to pick up a stick and throw it for the dog before he finally caught onto the idea that a beach and a dog could be fun. He could just be a boy at the beach.

We finally arrived at the lake. My feet and shoulders were a bit sore—more than I'd admit to my sons. The old man could keep up with them, right? I wasn't going to disappoint them.

I showed them how to pitch the tent, and we unrolled our sleeping bags and settled in. They brought water from the lake, and we learned how the water filter worked. Soon dinner was cooking.

I suggested they gather wood for a fire, and they brought back a strange assortment of wood and twigs. I could see that fire building and tending were skills they needed to learn. They were definitely out of their comfort zone.

The hike and the spectacle of the snowcapped, rugged volcanic peak, rising above the ridge on the other side of the lake, had sharpened their appetites. We watched the basalt-and-summer shrunken snow-fields turn pink in the setting sun. A few deer wandered through the camp, and we sat in silence, taking it all in.

The boys' mouths were agape as the deer wandered through, and an owl hooted in the forest, giving the place a nice, somber mountain mood. There was magic here, and they started to want to be part of it.

The next morning I woke up early and made my campfire coffee in silence. The thin air was chilly, even for August. Finally the water was hot, and I poured that first special cup of hot coffee and found a log by the lake to take my first sip. I looked over the lake, watching the mist rise a bit as the first glint of the morning sun struck the summit of the mountain.

I was in heaven. It simply didn't get better than this.

I heard a twig snap, and the younger boy sat down beside me. I poured him a cup too, and we just sat there, taking it all in.

"What are you doing?" he asked, his head cocked in wonder. *What is this crazy man doing here, just looking at the lake?* he must have wondered. *It's cold, and we're miles from the car, and we're stuck here for four more days!*

"Just enjoying the peace," I replied, amazed again at having to explain something that just seemed so matter of fact, a part of the nature of the experience. I'd never asked my dad that question because we just went camping, and the reasons for it all were buried deep in my genes.

He took his first sip of coffee, and we watched the morning sunlight work its way slowly down the mountain until the first rays hit the nearby trees and then finally the lake. It was about the most peaceful half hour you could hope for, and he took it all in, not moving a muscle. I could tell the magic of the mountain and the peace of the lake were finally getting to him.

He finally smiled.

"Are you having a good time, Son?" I asked.

"Yeah. I think I'm going to have a good week here."

What is my relationship with solitude?

It is profound and deep. It is an integral part of my daily routine and my spiritual practice.

Our culture is filled with data, noise, mayhem, and continual interaction. Yet it is in silence that I engage my creativity, strength, and empathy to deal with others.

More importantly, I engage my essence, my true self. It is lonely, but it has a positive connotation. I encounter myself, my energies, and the place where I access the energies of the universe.

This communion doesn't depend on a location but rather on a state of mind, a state of being.

We are human beings, not human doings. So I strive to "be," not "do"—to be congruent with my own nature, my own essence.

Loneliness isn't bad, nor is it antisocial. Being in loneliness empowers me, allows me to be fully engaged, to be fully present with myself.

When I am so renewed and reconnected, it is then that I am more fully prepared to be in the presence of other beings and continue my work as a "being."

I need time to contemplate, to fully absorb, and to fully experience my feelings. And when I am not, I am disconnected from myself. It is when I am so disconnected that I become lonely. My loneliness is being apart from self.

In solitude I am connected, I am nourished, and I am whole.

That week my sons learned about campfire building, cooking on a hiker's stove, blisters, and fishing. They learned about digging a hole to make a toilet and to appreciate a cold gulp of water after a hike—water that came from a creek.

And they learned about silence and the peace that comes from the wilderness, about finding happiness and contentment in their new-found manhood.

fourteen

The Power of Self-Love

I learn by going where I have to go.
—*Theodore Roethke*

Love.

We hear the word all the time—in songs, in conversations, on talk shows, in all of the self-help books. We celebrate it, we pursue it, we revel in it, and we continually define it. We hunt for it, we treasure it, and we lament when we lose it.

It's easiest to use in our language when we describe it and intellectualize it in terms of a pairing or within a family. For most of our conversations, that's where it stays: the verb and the noun through which we try to convey all the tensions, the anxieties, the joys, and the energies of those relationships.

Yet we don't define it very well when we apply those concepts to ourselves and our inner perceptions—our inner struggles with who we are inside.

Loving myself? Oh, that's a dark place often unexplored and rarely expressed or defined. It is easier by far to wrestle with the back and forth of a couple—two people, seeking the depth of love between them, emotional, with give-and-take, with "issues," with struggles. Looking at what two people do in their dance is easy to visualize. It's easy to spot the tensions and the good times, the familiar good paths, and the rocky, challenging paths in their journey together.

Even in writing this, it is easier for me to fall back on that familiar territory: the couple, the relationship, the marriage, the parent and child. Words have familiar meanings, and we have common ground with others in the discussion, in the thinking process.

Each person has that space where he or she has his or her own "stuff" maybe stacked and sorted neatly in the closet or thrown in a heap, not yet sorted out. The closet is dark, it is a bit disorganized, and it is kept shut. We don't want our friends to have much of a look inside, let alone be with ourselves on a bad day.

Going deep into me, I find a scary place, fraught with memories, old patterns of old relationships, and unresolved questions and crises. The personality in the closet isn't the stuff of romance, of couples "clearing the air" and "getting to know each other." No, the personality there is our real selves. It's not the one we get all showered and dressed up for the day at the office, the party, or maybe the lunch with a friend.

This is the guy who is there—in here—needing to sort stuff out at three in the morning when I wake from a "toss and turn" night, needing to open the closet a bit and sort through things.

I don't like looking in the mirror and deciding that a big part of the problem I'm having is what lies in the reflection. Yeah, you. I mean, me. The buttons have been pushed, and I've responded to something, and what I see just isn't very pretty. In fact, it's downright ugly. Otherwise I wouldn't be lying awake now, staring at the darkened ceiling, not wanting to look inside and pull open the closet door.

Every philosopher, every poet, every chanteuse throughout history calls us to look inside that closet and sort through the baggage of childhood, adolescence, relationships, work, marriage, children, friendships, and all the other experiences in life. Each one of us leaves something in the closet that is unresolved, unanswered.

Many of us never venture far into the closet, preferring not to deal with the conundrums of life, the mysteries of our own psychologies.

We use indifference, the throwing of ourselves into our work, our daily routines, or the lives of our children as a means of keeping the closet locked. Or we fall into the socially acceptable pathway of having a drink "to take the edge off" or "to relax." With the advent of chemistry and pharmaceuticals, we take a pill.

Watching the evening news in this day and age subjects us to a plethora of various pills that will "cure" the problem and take care of whatever may ail us. Western medicine looks to the regimen of symptom, diagnosis, and treatment—almost always a pharmaceutical concoction with a host of various side effects—to "get us back on track" to return to "normal."

The age-old approaches of meditation, prayer, nutrition, exercise, a meaningful life, and an active and rich social life are being rediscovered. They help us to get back in touch with ourselves and give us the permission we must feel, the tools we need, to yank open the closet door, even for just a bit, and look around, take stock, and ultimately bring a bit of order to it all.

We've had to rely on Freud and Jung and the whole realm of academic psychology to engage in what shamans and spiritual masters have known for millennia: our dreams and our spirituality are the tools we have to look inside the closet. We can use them to find order and calm and ultimately self-fulfillment.

This journey inward is all about loving ourselves. It's about knowing our inventory of experiences, of doubts, of conundrums, and of being sure of ourselves enough to know that each of us has the skills and the tools by which we can discover our inner strength, our inner power, and our inner peace.

There's a great deal of beauty in that closet, often covered up and hidden by the flotsam and jetsam of life and our fear of really seeing our inner beauty. We are afraid to accept our beauty and the wonder of our own very special selves. We can bloom, but we are afraid to nourish the buds from which the flowers can burst forth.

Theologians, philosophers, psychologists, and the friends in your life you turn to when life gets to be a bit too much all know this. The wise friend helps us to discover the forest for the trees—the big picture.

The concept of God offers spiritual calm, spiritual order, and acceptance, giving us a place and a foundation from which to build our house in this world. We welcome order; we welcome a system through which we can find our inner peace and our inner strength.

One concise expression of that spiritual safe haven within us and our key to opening that treasure chest are found in the Prayer of St. Francis of Assisi:

> Lord, make me an instrument of your peace.
> Where there is hatred, let me sow love.
> Where there is injury, pardon.
> Where there is doubt, faith.
> Where there is despair, hope.
> Where there is darkness, light.
> Where there is sadness, joy.
> O Divine Master,
> grant that I may not so much seek to be consoled, as to console;
> to be understood, as to understand;
> to be loved, as to love.
> For it is in giving that we receive.
> It is in pardoning that we are pardoned,
> and it is in dying that we are born to Eternal Life.
> Amen.

Bill W. expressed these concepts in his Twelve Steps, helping people who were struggling with alcoholism. His movement, Alcoholics Anonymous, caught on in the desperate times of the Great Depression, inspiring millions to take control of their lives and effectively deal with their addictions.

An essential component of AA is that the new practitioner of the Twelve Steps makes connection with a sponsor. The sponsor is an AA member who is active in the program and has developed a life of sobriety. The sponsor is a link to the fine art of practicing and living the Twelve Steps—a person who provides stability and strength to the new member. In essence, the sponsor is a mentor.

Mentorship is the key to many programs in many religious organizations. Life is hard, and the path to spiritual peace and self-love is often difficult. A mentor guides the way, offering guidance, experience, and a light along the way.

Mentorship is a powerful force in our spiritual journey toward self-love and self-esteem. The novice monk has an abbot for guidance and time to apprentice, has a process of growing, and has space for coming of age in his spiritual discipline. He also has a quiet, safe refuge from the vagaries of the world. Where there is quiet, there is space for reflection and a daily routine. The monastery offers the novice safety and structure and an orderly path to spiritual enlightenment and personal peace. It is a good place in which to open the closet and do some cleaning and straightening.

In many religions there are saints, people whose lives serve as inspiration—mentors, if you will—for how to cope with life and how to find inner peace and a union with God.

All faiths have stories of people who have become spiritually enlightened, who have literally seen the light and have found peace and acceptance. The story of Buddha's enlightenment is the journey of a man seeking to reconcile his life experiences and expectations with the realities of the world and making sense of all life offers.

In nearly all such stories, there are guideposts and mentors along the way, offering solace, comfort, guidance, and direction. This is mentorship as a holy mission.

In mentorship there is a time when the relationship becomes a vessel through which the outer layers of addiction, anger, acting out, retribution, and other expressions of self-doubt and self-loathing are peeled away, exposing a wound. There is blood, and there is pain. There is doubt and uncertainty.

During these times, the task of the mentor is to exercise strength and stability, and to provide a firm platform of guidance. It is not what the mentor says but more what the mentor does. We lead by example by how we live our own lives and deal with our own pain. From that experience comes wisdom.

When our partner in this great adventure shares his or her pain, how does the mentor respond to this great outpouring of pain and self-abusive words and conduct? Is there quiet acceptance of the condition and a subtle-yet-unwavering current of looking inward for the sufferer? Is there permission to go inside the closet and at least turn the light on?

The telling of one's own story becomes a powerful tool. The story of another's journey offers inspiration and comfort. The parables of

Jesus—simple stories with profound spiritual lessons—were rich teaching methods, and they remain so today.

Story is what we truly want to hear, and it is how we truly learn. We are the result of tens of thousands of years of society building, most of which was nourished around the campfire after a long and perilous day of hunting, of gathering, of sheer survival. Successes and failures were explored, and new ideas were discussed. There was comfort in being in the group, within the tribe, sharing the light and warmth of the fire. Dreams were shared, and tools to survive tomorrow's hunt were honed.

Stories are spiritual tools and ministry.

Today we tell the story not only in the pulpit but also at the church coffee hour, at lunch with a friend, in a phone call, in a text message, and in a Facebook posting. We tell the story around the dinner table and with a coworker at the office.

"We are an oral society," a noted writer said at a recent workshop.

Her successful book is really a story—a story we can share around the modern campfire at the mouth of the cave. Her writing draws us in, making us snuggle closer to the fire and listen to the weaving of the tale by the tribal storyteller, who imparts wisdom and hope.

As storytellers, we also need to tell our own stories—not only to others around the fire, but also to ourselves. In that storytelling we find the love we have for ourselves.

The mentor simply gives us the permission to find the words, take a deep breath, and open our mouths.

The mentor lets us love ourselves.

fifteen

The Power of One

It's the action, not the fruit of the action, that's important. You have to do the right thing. It may not be in your power, may not be in your time, that there'll be any fruit. But that doesn't mean you stop doing the right thing. You may never know what results come from your action. But if you do nothing, there will be no result.
—*Mahatma Gandhi*

Can I really make a difference in the world? Does what I do really matter?

The other day, I ran into a young man I'd worked with. We had long talks about his future. We became friends, and I was a cheerleader in his life. I watched him refocus in high school and graduate school. I walked with him and held his hand as he thought about college and enrolling.

A few years later, I watched him receive his community college diploma, laughing with him as he posed for a family picture, diploma in hand. His wife and his sister, now both in college, stood proudly beside him.

At the store he shared a photo of his new baby and his dream of a bright future—getting his bachelor's degree—which would create a bright future for him and his family.

"Thanks," he said quietly. "Without you pushing me, encouraging me, I wouldn't be where I am today."

A few weeks ago, I took a young man to a university, walked with him into the registrar's office to schedule his classes, and got him ready for fall term. We'd worked together last spring to get him admitted. We started the process to transfer all the credits he'd earned for his associate's degree, and he was ready to start his junior year. He'd been aiming for a bachelor's degree for a long time and was finally able to make the move into a four-year university, one that has an excellent program in his area of interest.

He'd been dragging his feet, not making the phone call to schedule his class registration, nor finishing other paperwork that needed to get done before he was really ready to begin classes. The plan was for me to drive him there, make a day of it, and celebrate his achievements. But he was dropping the ball, ignoring my increasingly less-than-subtle hints to take that drive and move on with his life.

I nudged, I prodded, and I waited. Procrastination and fear took over, even a bit of resentment toward me for being the quiet voice urging him forward, encouraging him to go live his dream. What was going on here?

Time was running out, and I spoke up, becoming direct, calling out for him to confront the elephant in the living room and get moving with his life. We met, finally, to have that hard conversation. We argued, we struggled, and we finally got to the heart of his struggle. We each teared up, our guts churning.

We named the elephant, and we argued some more. He asked me where he thought he'd be in a few years if he didn't go to college—if he didn't make that short trip to the university's registrar that week and get ready for the fall term.

I got blunt and painted a realistic picture.

"If you don't live your dream and if you don't work toward achieving your goals, life will be hard, and life will be disappointing. You will end up being disappointed in yourself. Is that what you want?"

This was turning into a difficult dance. Each of us struggled, trying to figure it out.

He admitted that he really did want to go to college, but the old voices—the voices of childhood that had always whispered that he wasn't good enough, that he wasn't deserving of success—were lately speaking loudly in his head.

I took a breath. It was my job to listen and be supportive—to be the good father he'd never had.

We refocused. We didn't dwell on "failure" and "I'm not good enough." Instead, we moved on, living in today. We looked toward the future—planning for it, taking real-time steps to get where he wanted to go.

I grabbed the car keys and his cold, sweaty hand, and I walked him to my car. Amazingly, at least to him, within an hour we were at the registrar's office at the university, organizing his schedule, planning for his graduation in two years. He registered for classes, accepted his healthy array of scholarships, and sent in his student loan application.

On the way out the door, we picked up his student body card and scheduled a time for him to meet his department head and double-check his class schedule to make sure he was on the right track with his major.

Along the way, every college staff person was courteous, informative, and dedicated to getting him enrolled and off to a good start. Each one of them took the time to take an interest in him, to focus on his needs, and to help him achieve his goals for the day and for the next two years of his life.

Each one of them was taking the time, being interested, and investing in him. He saw that in how they treated him, how they were living their day: caring about one other person, one at a time, with all their focus, all their energy, all their wisdom.

So it began: the new student and the teachers, the first lesson, building on the past and aiming at the future.

I learned again those powerful tools: being patient, understanding, listening. I had to put away my own ego, my own agenda, and just listen and be a caring dad. I learned again that real change happens one person at a time.

sixteen

Being a Macho Man—or Not

When we are really honest with ourselves we must admit our lives are all that really belong to us. So it is how we use our lives that determines the kind of men we are.

—Cesar Chavez

How do you win in the world today? What does it take to achieve victory?

We men are warriors, trained to be tough, rugged, and manly by the adults in our lives, by our exposure to television programming, by the world of sports, and by our dealings with the world. We are to be competitors, not giving in to pain or disappointment or loss. We must be winners; we must be conquerors. We must win at all costs.

The military recruitment posters, the beer ads, the atmosphere of the locker room and the ballpark—all these champion our role as being the best, being the champion. Those who win make the money, enjoy the fame, and win the prettiest gal. They are the ones being interviewed on TV, and their faces are the ones appearing on the sports page and on ESPN.

Yet real life isn't that way at all. Being the fierce competitive athlete or the warrior in the workplace, striving for victory, hardly resembles the classroom or the workplace, and it especially doesn't resemble our family life. Instead, in those mundane, everyday situations, we find happiness and real fulfillment by working together, supporting other people's work, and achieving the final product by using our talents of cooperation, give-and-take, and mediation. By finding common ground, by encouraging others' talents, the work gets done, family life flourishes, and our friendships deepen. This is the work of real men.

We don't keep score at work, and we don't keep checking the time clock and the record books at home. We don't keep track of the number of our friends or how often we give real support to those in need. Real success isn't a numbers game.

Our real power isn't honored in the record books or by the cheers in the locker room or the bar after the game. The real winners aren't the ones the TV personality interviews or the ones who have their pictures on the front page of the sports section.

The real achievements—the real power—come from the quiet, behind-the-scenes work. They come in the quiet words of encouragement, the few words of advice to the coworker or the upset child or the spouse who is having a tough day. The real achievements come from a warm hand on the other guy's shoulder as you let him know you care and that he can solve the problem and learn the difficult task.

The real work, the real achievement, is the opening up of one's heart and one's soul. It is to be vulnerable, soft, exposed. It is to know one's feelings and not be in judgment of one's emotions, one's thoughts, one's self. It is ultimately to be naked, stripped of pretension and expectations of others and expectations of yourself. When all that posing and strutting is stripped away, what is left is the real you: a beautiful child of God.

Being the mentor, being the whole, complete man, is letting the other guy know that you care, that he can change, that he is the one who has the power in his own life to make a difference and to go ahead in life. It is in letting people know they have the skills and the talents and that they can find the solutions. That is the real power—the power of encouragement—and our solid, steadfast belief in the ability of the other guy to pick up the right tool and take charge of his life.

The real power lies in building confidence and in letting others know you believe in them. It is in being the cheerleader, the advocate, and the mentor. It is the quiet conversation of encouragement over a cup of coffee or in a corner of an office hallway, letting them know you believe in them. It is in making a commitment to listen, to encourage, to nurture. No one is keeping score.

It is in those moments that we flex our muscles and strut our stuff. It is then that we are real men. It is those several minutes of true listening—the quiet nod, the firm handshake, the pat on the back—where your real manhood comes out. You aren't there for the glory; you are there because you are a friend, a believer, and a supporter.

In all that you are truly powerful. You are truly a man: a human and humane. You change lives, and you make a difference—a real difference.

seventeen

Superheroes and the Dalai Lama: Purging Violence from My Life

> *The Roots of Violence: Wealth without work, Pleasure without conscience,*
> *Knowledge without character, Commerce without morality, Science with-*
> *out humanity, Worship without sacrifice, Politics without principles.*
> —*Mahatma Gandhi*

I did some serious thinking after a week of watching a violent "super-hero" movie and listening to the Dalai Lama talking about changing how we look at the world around us, how we live with our family and neighbors, and how we can be peacemakers.

I spent a Saturday at an environmental summit in the presence of the Dalai Lama, along with ten thousand other people—people who cared enough about their spiritual lives and humankind's impact on the environment to spend a gorgeous spring day inside, listening and absorbing wisdom and spirituality not only from the spiritual leader of Tibet but also from other thought-provoking leaders.

I came away invigorated, stimulated by the sheer simplicity of their wisdom and their ideas to change how we live and what we are here on this planet to accomplish.

A few days earlier, I had gone to the movies with my wife, and I had sat through a showing of the latest superhero blockbuster. It was nearly two hours of loud explosions, terrorism, weapons gadgetry, and death.

Oh, the good guys "won" in the end, and all was right with the world, and all the violence and death were just "fantasy."

I'm not sure my mind could really tell the difference, and during the next few days, I felt disoriented, out of sorts, not in tune with whom I strive to be and how I want to live my life.

The contrast between watching the movie and listening to an inspiring talk about compassion and one's purpose in life, and how we can serve others, churned inside me. The two experiences, occurring a week apart, left me feeling incongruent, conflicted, not easily reconciled.

When I visit our local youth prison, I talk with young men who are locked up for six or seven years—men who have worked on their addictions, their anger, their rage, and the abuse they've experienced and inflicted on others. These are men who are trying to move on with their lives, trying to find some peace and some purpose for their rejuvenated, rehabilitated lives.

Violence and rage haven't suited them very well, and they are paying the price. Our society has come up with the simplistic solution of locking them up in prison, with a mandatory prison term and no incentive to earn time off for good behavior. Such thinking does its share in contributing to anger and rage and in making someone feel worthless, separated, distant from the community.

I suppose there is the argument that society is being protected and that the prisoners are being punished. Yet there are a lot of costs we are all paying and will pay in the future for such an approach to dealing with kids who've been neglected, abused—kids who have grown up without parents and in households ravaged by addiction and violence and indifference.

Does the possibility of seven years in prison really become a factor in the twisted insanity of drugs, neglect, abuse, and sexuality in a fourteen-year-old, whose brain has yet to achieve any rational degree of processing and controlling emotion? Somehow deterrence doesn't seem to be an effective argument for mandatory prison time for these menchildren—not in this highly sexualized and drug-promoting culture.

A friend of mine often says, "What we permit, we promote."

I often wonder what we could have accomplished in their lives if the 140-plus dollars a day taxpayers spend to keep each one of these young men in prison had been spent early in their lives so we invested in their childhood and offered hope, opportunity, and emotional support. Perhaps they might not have ended up here, watching the calendar, being a bit fearful of how they are going to cope with being out of prison, how they are going to manage their lives.

Not having a father in their lives is the norm with the young men I visit, and they feel physically abandoned, emotionally cut off, flawed. That hunger eats into them, into their souls.

During family visiting time on Mother's Day, only eight youth out of the seventy-five imprisoned there were visited by their families. As I visited with two young men, hearing more about their lives, their hopes, and their dreams—and hopefully instilling a little emotional support and healthy values as we sipped coffee and played a game—I looked at the empty tables, thinking of families not being there for their sons.

That is a form of violence in our world: not being there in that positive "good parent" sense, in the lives of young men.

Such violence is not far removed from the senseless Boston Marathon bombings or the gang-related shootings in New Orleans during their Mother's Day parade—shootings that injured nineteen people who were out for a day with their families, celebrating a bit of parenting, a bit of maternal love and nurturance.

There is a simple reason we have gangs in our country: they offer the feeling of family, the belonging young men crave. There is a place for them, a role to play. They fit in.

And that blockbuster "superhero" movie? It remained the most popular movie on Mother's Day weekend.

I can understand why all the ticket holders for the superhero movie may not be as eager to spend their time listening to an elderly Tibetan monk share his thoughts about human compassion and how we can change our intentions and our attitudes—and thereby change how we live and how our community functions. After all, there aren't any robotic fantasy gadgets and special effects, no exploding bombs or crashing planes, no bullet-defying armor to keep us on the edge of our seats. There aren't any computer-animated soundtracks or a plot where the good guy destroys the bad guys in a burst of light and color and noise that's loud enough to shake my seat.

Instead there is a calm, thoughtful voice and a thoughtful, soul-feeding discussion about who we really are and what we can truly be capable of if only we would use our brains and hearts.

I'm now going to spend my time a bit differently—thinking about compassion, living my real values, and spending a lot less time in the movie theater or keeping up with the latest headline news shows.

eighteen

In the Listening: The Real Agenda

*...I remember thinking how often we look, but never see...we listen, but never hear...
we exist, but never feel. We take our relationships for granted. A house is only a place.
It has no life of its own. It needs human voices, activity and laughter to come alive.*
—Erma Bombeck, A Marriage Made in Heaven: Or Too Tired for an Affair

I should never assume I'm in charge of the agenda.

The other day I had a visit with one of my young friends at the local prison. I have been mentoring him, and he's been teaching me for quite a while. Visiting day was turning out to be the best day of the week for me on a lot of different levels.

I had our time all planned out. I brought food, some of his favorites, and coffee. (This part of the prison is "camp," so I can bring in store-bought food.) I brought my guitar and planned to play a game. I even laid out in my mind what we'd talk about as we ate and played the game. Silly me, thinking I'd be in charge of our time.

When I arrived, he didn't even open the bag from the restaurant. He barely sipped the special chocolate frappe I'd brought in. My guitar stayed in its case, and it was obvious he had a lot on his mind. His first words pushed me into the nearest chair, and he took command of our time, his eyes sparkling with the determination to speak his mind.

He talked and told me stories about his life, his family, and his fears. I heard about his grandma, his most challenging wrestling meet, and how his coach believed in him. The coach was the first man who'd ever thought he could do anything in his life.

The restaurant food grew cold; there was a different hunger in the room today—one burgers and fries wouldn't satisfy.

I heard about his best friend shooting someone at school and what it was like to watch that and hear the gunshots in his high school hallway, what it was like to turn around and see his friend firing the gun and the other guy falling and bleeding. Then he shared how he helped to get the gun away when the magazine was finally empty and how it fell, clanging on the hard linoleum floor, next to the blood.

I had to remember to breathe as his words quietly tumbled out—words without emotion. He was just relating the events, him being a reporter of what had gone on as he watched a murder.

He took me there, his words painting a picture of his fear and his empathy for his friend and explaining why his friend's anger had boiled over into gunfire. He didn't cry; he just spoke, his voice firm, the sentences turning into page-long paragraphs. I wondered whether anyone had ever heard this story, even after the cops arrived a few minutes later and took his friend to jail, leaving him in that long, cold hallway next to the bullet-riddled body, the empty magazine, and the blood.

His eyes told me it wasn't my time to ask, only to listen.

I could only nod, later occasionally offering a full sentence of empathy and understanding. His words tumbled out, keeping a steady pace, as the hand on the wall clock spun around—once, twice, and half again.

Finally he took a deep breath.

"I guess our time's up now. Can you come next week?" he said quietly, unfazed by his two-and-a-half-hour monologue, his story of murder and loneliness and the loss of a friend.

"Sure," I said, nodding and giving him a hug. He hugged back, bear-like, taking the sack of cold burgers with him.

"I'll heat these up in the microwave. Thanks."

When I got home, I took a walk in the autumn afternoon sunshine and looked at the colors of the leaves falling from the trees and the last of the summer flowers, those that had survived the first few nights of frost. The air was still; the rays of the setting sun were still warm on my skin.

There were no birds, no insects—not even a breeze in the dying, yellow leaves on the maple tree, as if the world knew I'd had enough listening for a while and needed to let all that settle in, to find a place for what I'd heard that afternoon.

I heard his stories again in that silence and let his tales sink deep into my soul. In all that, I realized I'd been given the gift of knowing him better and letting him finally be free to tell his stories and find his own way.

nineteen

Blowing Up

Let today be the day you finally release yourself from the imprison-
ment of past grudges and anger. Simplify your life. Let go of the poi-
sonous past and live the abundantly beautiful present... today.
— *Steve Maraboli*

"I blew up. I lost it," my friend said, grinning.

It was such a relief for him: exploding in rage, screaming, carrying on. In a few minutes, the prison staff had wrestled him to the ground, secured his flailing hands with handcuffs, and injected some Benadryl to quiet him. He'd earned his twenty-four hours in the "muser," the safe room where he could regroup and come to grips with his rage.

He'd had a hard day.

His phone call with his mom had ended in an argument and the same empty promises she'd been making for a while. He'd been fired from his work-crew job, as he was horsing around and disrespecting the task at hand.

His primary staff person tried to talk to him about his attitude and his last phone call with his mom. That talk, with a guy who brings him pizza once in a while as a reward for good work, didn't go well.

He'd also wound up his second go-around with his sex offender treatment, taking another run through all that life-challenging and life-changing work. With his medication changed and his increasing matu-rity, he'd been able to grasp the concepts more easily this time around and apply them to his life. He'd finally been able to see his childhood and his family life for what it really was.

A few weeks ago, his beloved grandfather had passed away. His passing hadn't been unexpected. My friend said it was actually a relief, given his grandfather's declining health and inability to live in his house. The death of his grandmother a few months ago had added to his grandfather's sadness and loneliness.

They were about the last of his dad's family, and there was a big emptiness in my friend's heart. Life with dad hadn't been easy. There had been a lot of alcohol, drugs, violence, and anger. When his dad had died when my friend was fifteen, a lot of unfinished business had punched him in the gut. He sometimes referred to his dad's death as a suicide, sometimes a drug overdose, sometimes a heart attack. He was the guy who was there, who called the ambulance, who watched his dad die as the EMTs tried their best.

He went to live with Mom, not that she wanted him. She and the boyfriend were busy with the bottle and the pipe, and they didn't need a teenage boy in the house. But he had no place else to go.

He's never had it easy. He's never enjoyed peace and a sense of place in this world. Life has always been a struggle, and he's been pushed into the insanity of drugs, alcohol, violence, prostitution, and sexual chaos. School became a joke, and he was sidelined and pushed through, grade after grade, and medicated so that teachers didn't have to deal with him. He was trash.

Mom pimped him out and arranged a lot of drug- and alcohol-infused "dates," which led to his arrest and prison.

It was one way to get him away from Mom and from his dancing around the fringe of the local gangs and criminal element; it was one way to get him off the streets. Going to prison saved his life. He's told me that several times, and he is right.

Now he's completed high school, he's completing his sex-offender treatment, he's been clean and sober for five years, and he's able to focus on his needs and his future. His social skills have grown, so he can live in peace with others and learn to take care of himself.

Still, last week was a huge milestone. Deep inside him, the anger about his childhood and his family has festered and stewed for his entire life. There are a lot of unresolved conflicts and emotions, and his limited contact with his family hasn't gone far in settling those. He's able to see a healthy alternative to all that chaos now, and that brings his anger about what he endured as a kid to an even higher boil.

I've played my role in that, too. I've been coming to visit him for two years. Every week we have coffee and talk. We talk about his work and his studies, about life in prison. We talk about his childhood a bit and his growing passion for his Native American roots; we talk about figuring out who he really is. He sets the agenda each time we visit, and sometimes the topic goes deep and hard.

I've challenged him just by showing up, being dependable, speaking quietly, and gently accepting him, warts and all. Knowing that I don't have to show up and be in his life has stymied him. I'm not a staff person. I'm not a prison guard or teacher or counselor. I just show up and talk.

I don't blow up. I don't manipulate him. I don't call him names. I do my best not to be critical or to put him down. He's had enough of that for several lifetimes.

I'm a cheerleader here—quietly and consistently pushing him a bit, believing in him, and celebrating the good things he's doing. Playing that role, I've befuddled him on many occasions, showing him that he's worthy and decent deep inside.

Over a year ago, he has struggled with writing about his offense and the impact it had on the victim and with trying to see the abuse from her point of view. His writing was a big part of his treatment work—the hardest part.

That was a big rock in the road, as he'd been sexually abused, too, as well as beaten and neglected and screamed at. He wrote a great essay on empathy and then wrote more about his life, using another name and turning it into fiction. That novella gave his pain some distance—space where he could deal with the pain.

This work went on for months, and there were a lot of times when he cried and threw his hands up; the enormity of this emotionally draining work overwhelmed him. I didn't judge him, and I didn't berate him for not sticking with the "schedule" of getting that work done.

He was digging deep and opening and healing some awful and infected wounds. He was taking his time with it—taking care when opening every door in his house of horrors—but only when he was ready for what was inside.

I waited. I wouldn't bring up the work unless he did. When he talked, I listened. I didn't play editor, critic, or judge. Oh, I cried sometimes. The stories that came out were beyond Steven King's imagination. This was his reality, and he was in charge of peeling back the layers and getting down to the awful core.

A year ago, we celebrated his birthday, an ordinary event for most of us. But at twenty-one, he'd never had a birthday party. He was able to invite his friends, and my wife and I brought in a cake and some ice cream, party hats, birthday plates, and napkins. We had presents and told jokes and laughed and sang "Happy Birthday."

He was nearly speechless. He'd doubted the idea that we would actually throw a birthday party for him. When it came, he quickly slipped into his twelve-year-old boyishness and took it all in.

The birthday party helped. It brought him in touch with his inner-boy sweetness, and some healing went on. Silently, we all gave him permission to be a boy, have a party, and enjoy himself just for who he was. After that his treatment work moved ahead, and he was able to complete his writing.

When that was done, he was a little shy in telling me that the big project was, at last, finished. He let out a smile, but he looked to me for approval.

I put it right back at him.

"This was your project, not mine. This was your work, not mine. You get the credit for all this," I said. "Not me. This is your achievement."

He knew that, of course, but he needed me to say the words.

We celebrated then with some ice cream. He let it slip that he'd never celebrated an accomplishment in his life with anyone. Having ice cream just because you did something hard was something new.

It was another thing for me to cry about as I drove home from our visit.

Last week when he blew up, it was a big deal. He'd been dancing around the monster in his basement for his entire life. His treatment and his writing finally gave him permission to put on his armor and deal with the monster. His monster had lots of faces and lots of evil and darkness. Its demands and screams have filled his ears his entire life.

Last week he went to war, taking on the monster and calling it out of his basement.

"I'd never fought it before—never let myself get angry and take it on," he told me. "But it was time. I wasn't going to take it anymore, and I was going to fight him."

When the six burly staff persons struggled with him, putting him on the ground and handcuffing him and letting him scream for a half hour, he was winning the battle.

"It felt good to struggle, to fight back. I knew they were helping me," he said.

He'd never fought back before, taking the beatings from his dad, taking the indifference and manipulation and pimping out of his young sexual self in silence and acceptance. He didn't contest the criminal charges or the seven-year sentence. He didn't cry much when his grandparents died or when his brother was first busted for heroin. It was all just how his miserable, worthless life was.

It was, after all, what he deserved. His dad had said he was worthless, a good-for-nothing. That must have been true. No one ever had said anything different.

He'd never given voice to his grief before—to the grief of a lost childhood, of abandonment, of the death of family members he loved and feared. He'd never cried before over his younger brother, now living on and off the streets, dabbling in heroin and sex and petty crime. He'd never screamed before about being locked up for seven years, about the sex party his mom had arranged, and about his empty teenage life.

He makes fifty cents an hour in prison. When his mom asked him last year for money, he never raised his voice.

"I'd be dead now. I'm sure of it," he told me a few weeks ago, giving thanks that he was in prison and had found the help he needed.

He walks more easily now, and a slight grin flashes across his face, even when he is being serious. There's light in his eyes, and his shoulders are thrown back, a little pride showing in his face. He's grown about four inches these last two years, too, and he brags about his running and weight lifting, about how his biceps are bigger now.

I'm sure there's some cleanup work to do down in the basement of his young life. But the monster is on the run now, no longer the king of the underground. My friend has found his spear and axe, and he has gone into battle, committed to victory.

twenty

Ritual

*He remains a boy, not because he wants to, but because no one has
shown him the way to transform his boy energy into man energies.*
—Robert Moore, King, Warrior, Magician, Lover

If we don't initiate the boy, he will burn down the culture.
—Michael Meade

If you haven't noticed, in our culture there's no clear line between boyhood and youth, and youth and manhood. Oh, we have laws that establish when men can vote, go to war, or drive a car.

Biology gives us puberty, but we shove that change to the back room,
and we don't talk about coming of age or becoming a man.

When my stepson celebrated his fourteenth birthday, I gave him a
razor. It is what my dad gave me when I turned fourteen, and I thought
it was an act of symbolism and recognition of his oncoming masculinity
and his ability to grow a few hairs on his chin.

Yet the embarrassment and chagrin I got in response was really
society saying, "What are you making a big deal out of anyway?"

Yet it is a big deal: boys becoming men. It is a huge step, a leap into
adulthood and away from childhood.

In Hispanic culture, the daughter's fifteenth birthday is a time for
a party, for fancy dresses, music, presents, and a gigantic family event
that brings in all the neighbors, all the community.

"Look here. Our beautiful daughter is becoming a woman. We celebrate and honor her, and we celebrate the beauty of women."

Yet the dominant culture ignores these transitions. We have going to the high school prom, and we have passing the driver's test.

We have high school graduation, but a lot of kids don't go to the ceremony. In our community, even if you complete high school, you don't get to walk across the stage and have your name read aloud to all the parents and relatives unless you've completed a senior project. So a lot of kids don't even get that recognition.

Yet ritual and initiation have been part of human life ever since there were human societies. Caves and tombs have revealed jewelry, musical instruments, paintings, and ceremonial garb.

Every "primitive" culture on this planet has established customs for the naming of a child, the onset of puberty, the welcoming of the new warrior into manhood, the beginning of menstruation, and the marriage of a young man and a young woman. Birth and death, and all that is between, had a time for recognition and honor.

Bar mitzvahs have enjoyed a revival lately, simply because people need a ceremony in which the community takes notice that a boy is now a young man and is now responsible and mature.

Australian Aborigines celebrate the walkabout; Native Americans celebrate their youth by returning from a vision quest. African tribes celebrate a similar event, and the entire village turns out to bid them adieu on a great adventure and celebrate their entry into manhood when they return.

It is a big deal. A very big deal.

Trust Walk

When he was a teenager, one of my sons struggled with his spirituality—his question of whether the world was simply random chaos or whether maybe there was a divine entity out there, or in here, that gives it all some structure, some rationality.

He couldn't buy into organized religion or, as he put it, "some imaginary friend." He was a questioner and a thinker, but he struggled with a nagging sense that simple logic and reason didn't provide a satisfying answer either.

The question began to consume him, and he wondered what manhood was. Part of him was being tugged back into childhood, and a big part of childhood was something he simply hadn't experienced, given his crazy upbringing (or, as I would call it, the "non-upbringing").

One day I took him on a walk through the backyard. We did a trust walk, and I had him blindfold me.

"Take me on a walk," I said. "Guide me and keep me safe."

He was so reluctant, so fearful.

"I trust you," I said. "You will keep me safe."

Off we went. I showed him how to take my arm over his. I was blind, and he was my eyes. He was the guide, and I was the child. He was the dad, and I was the son.

He was a masterful guide, and we walked ever so slowly and cautiously along the garden paths, up and down the hill, around shrubs and paving stones, and around a tree.

He was astonished that I'd trust him, and yet I had no fear. He could sense I had no fear. He was, after all, my son, and my son was now a man. The transformation in our roles was subtle yet empowering. I could sense a change in his energy. Manhood was in bloom there in the garden that afternoon.

When we were done, he took off my blindfold, a big grin across his face.

"Is it my turn?" he asked, a bit impishly.

"You betcha," I replied, putting the blindfold across his young, beaming face.

As we walked through the yard and the garden, my hand and arm under his arm now, I talked about intuition and wisdom, experience and confidence.

He laughed, chuckling at the thought of being led, blind, through the garden outside his bedroom window—he and his old man shuffling through the plants and stepping-stones and going around the tree again.

The summer afternoon sun was waning, the light catching in the stubble along his jaw. I looked at him. He was a man now, this boy-child who had come into my life only a few years ago—beaten, weary, and leery of this guy who was going to be some kind of father to him.

Oh, that word wasn't a good one for him. "Biological dad" was a scarce commodity in his life, and mom had a number of boyfriends, whose actions with him and his brother had run the gamut from indifference to beyond abusive. On our first day together, I was Neal. He was comfortable with that, and he never called me "Dad" except to his friends. I had to earn that title, though. It wasn't one he'd ever think of giving out lightly.

"I'm always here for you, Son," I said, my arms around him now, pulling him in for a bear hug. "I'm so proud of you."

A big breath whooshed out of his lungs. He was home now, and he was really himself.

His shoulders were relaxed now, and there was the old twinkle in his eyes. He chuckled; he laughed. He was at ease with himself, comfortable in his own skin.

The Talking Stick

In my men's group, we begin our meetings with one of us lighting sage and smudging each of us as we enter the house. The bundle of dried sage leaves is lit, and one man wafts the smoke around the head and shoulders, and down the arms, torso, and legs of each of the other men. This is an act of purification, a symbol of cleansing away the worries and tasks of the day, centering ourselves in the moment, preparing each of us for ceremony, and togetherness.

We slowly turn clockwise—the direction of male energy—and enter the room, taking our seats around the living room.

One man lights a candle in the small sculpture of a group of figures in a circle. The sculpture sits on the floor, always in the center, a sign of being together.

We stand, arms around each other, and come together physically and now spiritually. One man begins a low note, deep in his chest, and we all join in, not seeking harmony. The notes vary and move up and down the scale until we are out of breath and the room has been filled with our collective energy and noise. We are one, and we have made the world aware of that.

The leader for the evening picks up a polished stick, its twisted grain beautifully sanded and varnished to a smooth sheen. It is time for us to begin. Whoever speaks holds the stick. It is passed around the room from man to man, always in a clockwise direction.

Only one man speaks. The rest of us are called by the stick to listen. It is a meeting of listening, of paying attention, of focusing our energies on the man who is speaking from his heart.

On the way home, I am always amazed at the power of such a simple process: a time of simply coming together and listening to one man, one man at a time. We sit around a flame in a circle—all equal, all together.

And the work that is done there is one of the most powerful tasks I can hope to undertake.

Communion

In my town the real church is the potluck supper. There are so many churches that the church section of the yellow pages goes on for four pages—a bigger category than anything else around here. They all have their morning service, their church school, their afternoon service, their evening service, their Wednesday service, the ladies' circle, the men's club, the choir practice, and whatever else they can come up with.

But the real communion, the real holy sacrament that is taken in this town, is the potluck. It's not a real meeting unless there's food. If you don't advertise that there's food, you'll be looking at a lot of empty chairs.

But even if there are just cookies and coffee, more folks will show up. It's just the nature of the beast.

Weddings, funerals, service clubs, subcommittees—they all require food. I'm not sure whether some groups would exist if they weren't noteworthy for the dinner they put on during their special day of the year on the community calendar.

As we gather, we seem to talk to each other and get the work done only if we have a paper plate in one hand, a napkin stuck under the plate, and a cup of coffee in the other hand. This setup eliminates a lot of needless handshaking, and so we greet each other with a nod and a mumbled greeting through teeth that have just bit into a really good casserole, salad, sandwich, or a famous dessert by one of the best cooks in town.

We don't call this a ritual, but it is. We are not only feeding our bellies; we are also feeding our community's soul.

When my friend, Father Ray, died, there was an overflow mass at his church, and when I tasted the wafer and the wine, I was reminded of the many good times I'd had with him. I remembered the food and the blessings of the assembled group the food and fellowship had nourished.

We ate after the mass, of course, and that was the real communion in the church that day. We told Father Ray stories, we laughed, we shared our grief, and we ambled home, feeling better, feeling together.

Communion occurs around the dinner table with the plate of cookies you bake and take to the kids gathered in the basement on a Friday night. You watch their eyes grow big when you open the door with a big plate of homemade cookies in your hands, and the cookies are still hot from the oven.

Communion is love and community.

Hugs

One of my newest friends is a young man in prison. One of his teachers and one of his counselors asked me to start up a relationship with him, to befriend him. I sent him a Christmas card, and he sent me one back, and so it began.

Mentoring, of course, usually comes unexpectedly. You need to be ready for it when it knocks on the door.

We took baby steps—writing letters—and then he put me on his visitors' list.

I show up at the prison door every Sunday afternoon, waiting there with some parents, grandparents, and a few uncles and aunts, waiting to walk through the metal detector and take our places around plastic tables in the main hall of the youth prison. It is a big room—institutional, cold, and heartless.

A room off to the side is where we can go for coffee and snacks. After we order and pay, another inmate will bring our order to our table. Other than the food, the place is pretty sterile.

The young man and I sit across from each other. One time we played cards, but mainly we just talk. Well, actually he talks, and I do most of the listening. He's got twenty years of not talking to catch up on and three more years of his sentence to serve. We have plenty of time.

We've gotten into some pretty deep subjects, like the crime that brought him here, his family, his father's death, his sister's imprisonment, his brother's addictions, his addictions, his anger. There's a lot there, and sometimes he has to skate around the wounds. They are still open and bleeding, and the pain is pretty intense.

When things get tough, he bumps his fist against mine, and I bump back.

"Yeah, buddy, I'm listening. I'm here for you," I say with my fingers, skin against skin. "Go deep. Go deep."

As the second meeting was ending and we were standing up, I asked him whether I could hug him. I hug everyone. Hugs are free. Hugs are really needed in this world. A hug does more for a person than most anything else.

He stepped back a bit, giving me the deer-in-the-headlights look.

"Ah, ah...I don't know," he stammered. "I'll have to ask my counselor."

OK. I'll wait until next time, I thought. I'd struck a nerve, an old wound. I'd better slow this down. This guy isn't ready for that kind of human touch in this world.

I could sense he thought a hug might be a good thing, but there was a lot going on with him beneath the surface.

Time would tell. I'll see where this goes.

The next meeting went well, and he talked a lot about heart words, feeling words. He's one to give me the abstract, intellectualized word for something going on with him, but what about the real flesh-and-blood words, the words that are all about nerve endings and the emotions in the lower, reptilian part of the brain and the emotional brain? Well, no. I'm not going there.

Actually, he may not be able to go there yet. There's a lot crammed inside there that isn't ready to come out yet—some wild tigers and trumpeting elephants that aren't quite ready to walk into the harsh, bright lights in this room.

That's OK; I'll wait him out. We have a long time.

But then, as we stood at the end of our session, he walked over and gave me a hug. Oh, not a bear hug, but a decent, full arm-around-the-back hug. I hugged him back.

We had hugged. That was enough. I'd call it a victory for the day. We'd made some progress.

When I was a kid, my family didn't hug. We barely shook hands, and that was only when relatives came to visit and all the men went through the ritual of shaking everyone else's hand.

My wife's family loved to hug. Everyone hugged me the first time they met me. They hugged me when I came in, when I left, and whenever they felt like hugging. It was contagious, and I found I loved it; I couldn't get enough of it.

I started hugging my men friends. They hugged back. They loved it. We started hugging in public. That was nearly a scandal. We went on a retreat one weekend to do some writing, drinking wine, reading, and mainly talking about our lives and our struggles with relationships. One guy suggested that we change our culture just a bit by hugging in public. We could be real men and still hug in public.

Really? We could?

Yeah, we could.

We did. Soon, other guys hugged—just a bit—and it caught on, just a bit.

Times have changed, and people hug a lot more these days.

But the people who really need hugs? It's not so easy. Someone has to show them it's OK to hug, and then it just becomes something you do.

You can even hug someone in prison. Really.

Initiation

Other cultures show young men how to find God, how to be in communion with God, and how to be comfortable in nature in that search.

Other cultures let men become men as a natural thing, as something celebrated and honored. Other cultures invite boys into the men's lodge, teach them manly things, and welcome them into rituals and celebrations so that becoming a man is seen as a joyous event, a recognition of honor and achievement.

Young men are starved for this, and their malnutrition for such rites is also starving our culture and the souls of young men. When our young men are hungry, they will try to find other nourishment through drugs, violence, sex outside of love, and gangs. And their rage will burn down the village.

It is time we met this famine head-on and provided a way for young men to become men, to learn the honor of being a man, to be accepted into the ranks of manhood, and to find community and honor, dignity, and respect. They are lost, but they want to be found.

We must find them, and we must bring them home.

twenty-one

The Rock of Resentment

Let today be the day you stop being haunted by the ghost of yester-
day. Holding a grudge and harboring anger/resentment is poison to
the soul. Get even with people...but not those who have hurt us, for-
get them, instead get even with those who have helped us.
— *Steve Maraboli, Life, the Truth, and Being Free*

He spoke of his anger, of raging inside, and of his feelings about his family, his childhood, the place where he was now, and what he struggled with. His eyes flashed, his voice strong and energized as he shared what was deep in his heart: the pain and the success.

"I've found a place to put all that, all my resentment," he said, tears welling up, his voice quivering.

It was his resentment rock.

"I give it all to the rock, every day, so I can sleep at night, so I have a place for all this," he said. "This morning, it broke. It's in two pieces now."

Silence filled the room. Everyone felt the tension as the rock broke, imagining that moment in his life.

Someone in the group asked him how he felt now—now that the rock of resentment had been broken.

"Oh, I'm free. The pressure is off. The tension is gone. Relief, I guess. Yeah, relief. All that resentment that was inside me, and now is inside the rock, is gone. It went away. I just feel lighter now," he said, one tear making its way down his young face. "I can move on now."

Later, when we had finished our conversations as a group, he talked to a woman. She had spoken in our group about a place she was making in her garden, a place to grieve, and an offering vessel she had made. It was a place where people could come to pray and leave an object, a symbol of their loss, their grieving. It was a place of honoring one's grief and the memories of good times and hard times. It was a place to honor what goes on deep in our hearts.

"Could you put this there?" he asked. "I want you to take the rock and put it there so I can let it be. I need a place to leave the rock—a place for all my resentment to be."

He took the two pieces of the rock out of his pocket, showing us how the two pieces fit, jagged edge to jagged edge. He let me hold them. The rocks felt heavy, my fingers sensing the burdens they contained.

His hands trembled as he put the two pieces in my hand. A large whoosh of air escaped from his chest.

"It's time to let all that go and move on with my life," he whispered, tears soaking into my shirt.

twenty-two

A Letter to Little Dave

In a futile attempt to erase our past, we deprive the community of our healing gift. If we conceal our wounds out of fear and shame, our inner darkness can neither be illuminated nor become a light for others.
— Brennan Manning, Abba's Child: The Cry of the Heart for Intimate Belonging

"Big" Dave is in prison for sexual assault. His childhood was chaos, riddled with alcohol, drugs, violence, gangs, one parent who died, and one parent who couldn't parent. His formal education was dumbed down, and he was passed from one grade to the next so that the "system" wouldn't have to address his dyslexia and his antisocial acting out.

As I'm talking to Dave in prison, he tells me he's writing to "Little Dave," his younger self, a boy who is nine years old. He finds in that process that he has some wisdom, some insight. It is safe to do this, too. There's some distance, some emotional insulation, in writing to "someone else."

He signs his letter to his younger self, "Empathy."

It is my turn to write to "Little Dave."

> Dear Dave,
>
> You don't know me yet, but someday, when you are a young man, you will meet me, and we will spend time together each week, just talking and learning about each other.

When it is my time to meet you, you will be a strong and brave young man. You will be in a safe place, away from turmoil and chaos. There will be order in your life, and your life will have structure.

You will spend a lot of your time learning about yourself, your emotions, and your ability to learn new things. You will be catching up on your schoolwork. You'll like this.

When you will know me, you will be finishing up your high school work, and you will graduate. You will talk about college and the future, and when you do, you will look happy and have a smile on your face.

You will be a lean man, and you will have lost a lot of weight. You won't be eating McDonald's food any more, and you will be wearing "skinny" clothes. Still, you will worry about how you look and how other people will see you. In the past, you have worried about this a lot.

When I begin to know you, you will be exploring your own mind and your own creativity. You will draw a lot, and you will show me your drawings, and you will be proud of yourself.

It will be hard to be proud of yourself, because for so long you have learned that you should not be proud of yourself and that you are not worthy of your own love. But later you will realize that this is not true and that this is not a healthy way to think.

You will have many experiences before you meet me. Some of those experiences will be sad, and many experiences will be scary. But you will get through those experiences and those feelings. When you get to my town to live, you will feel safe enough about life to begin to tear down your walls and give yourself permission to accept yourself and learn about yourself.

You will begin to like to change and to grow. This will be a good thing for you. You will know that.

You will show me lots of things about yourself: how you love to write, how you love to draw, how you love to read and learn new ideas and have new experiences.

You will find that you are a very special person. You are unique. You have unique gifts to offer the world.

You have always been a giver. You give unselfishly. When I know you, you will be able to also accept gifts from others, just for the sheer joy of giving and receiving. You will not be expected to give anything back when you get these gifts. The only expectation is that you accept the gifts and make good use of them. Over time, you will give to others in the same way.

Don't be anxious to grow up. We all grow up. Find parts of your childhood that you really enjoy and be able to laugh and have fun. When you are twenty, you will learn again how it is to be a child and to laugh and play and enjoy learning. You will learn again to love yourself.

Your friend in the future,

Neal

twenty-three

Naming Our Demons and Letting Go

Inside us all are pieces of that which makes the negative. Demons are neither good nor bad. Like you, they have many facets. It is that inner essence, or drive, if you will, that we all have that guides us through our lives. Sometimes those voices that drive us are whispered memories that live deep inside and cause us such pain that we have no choice except to let it out and to hurt those around us. But at other times, the voice is love and compassion, and it guides us to a gentler place. In the end, we, alone, must choose what path to walk. No one can help us with it. (Menyara)
— *Sherrilyn Kenyon, Bad Moon Rising*

I stood guard, looking east, my back to the breeze off the ocean and the flame-red sunset. Only the half of the moon and scattered clouds filled the sky. Soon it would be dark. The stars of autumn would reveal themselves, and Orion, the warrior, would again hold his shield against the demons of the dark.

Flames crackled behind me. My soul brother spoke to the stars, offering the agonies and the traumas of his life into the flames, purifying his soul as his life of tears entered the fire. Words were spoken, prayers were offered, and I could feel his soul lightening, his burdens easing. His energy tonight was powerful and filled our place on this beach with his strength, his soul work.

The rest of us stood silent, awed by his courage, his spirit work. The voice of my soul and those of my brothers around him joined him in his work, giving him our strength and our love. He's a Vietnam vet, and he asked us to surround him and be his honor guard as he dug deep into his own personal hell.

The demons of my own pain walked here, too, and I took in the energy of spirit and girded my loins for my own battles, my own challenges. For my brother and my fellow guards were with me tonight in my own battle, my own struggles. We were together, and I felt myself able to put down my own shield a bit and find comfort in the support of my brothers as I, too, waged battle and burned my own agonies in the bonfire lit by my brother.

He lit a piece of kindling. The smell of the sage and the cedar and the sweet grass mixed with the cleansing air from the ocean, its salt and its purity finding their way into the pit of my guts, the place where my soul keeps its wounds. I breathed deeply and let the poisons and the pain go. Release, renewal. Again. Yes, again. Each breath a new release, a new cleansing.

The knots in my shoulders—the ones I don't know exist until I can find release—unties themselves, and I was at ease. My blood, filled with the oxygen of the ocean and the cleansing of the smoke from the fire, brought new life and energy, and the tension was gone.

I looked into the eyes of my brother, he who has wrestled with his demons tonight, called them out, and named them. I saw his renewal, his release, his peace.

In the naming of them and in the giving up of them, the agonies lose their power over our souls. We can cut their chains, and we can move on and be free.

In his work tonight, I, too, was released. I was eased. I was renewed.

twenty-four

Taking on a Big Issue and Crawling out of the Bottle

It is not because things are difficult that we do not dare; it is because we do not dare that they are difficult.

—Seneca

Every two months, about thirty folks shuffle into the meeting room, sitting in every other chair, not wanting to look at the four or five of us sitting in the big chairs behind the table in front. No one wants to be there.

It's Wednesday night, and there's always someplace they'd rather be. But the judge on their DUI said they'd better show up or go to jail. They pay their fifty bucks in the hallway and check off their names on the list that will be sent to the judge the next morning.

It's just another requirement of the process.

The four or five of us speaking tonight at the local DUI victim impact panel have been doing this gig for years. I'm into my twenty-first year—not that there's much joy in this, though I do enjoy the companionship of my fellow speakers, getting together for dinner beforehand and visiting with them.

My stomach is usually in a knot all day, and I know I won't sleep very well that night, with my head sorting through all the stories my fellow speakers tell—of dead bodies on the side of the road, of how they go about telling families that someone died because of drunk driving. And there's the awful story of how a woman has been emotionally torn to shreds over and over again, because of a drunk who killed her brother.

One of the nicest cops in town tells us about watching his brother breathe his last, about telling his mom and his brother's kids about that night when his brother got drunk, tried to drive the back road home, and didn't make it.

That's a bad enough tale—enough to add another cup of stomach acid to the mix—but he goes on. I always wish he would stop the story right there. But he doesn't. He talks about how he and his wife raised his brother's kids as their own and how life changed for everyone because his brother decided to drive home after too many beers.

I hear those stories again and again, and I tell some of my own—about how drunk driving has kicked my life around and how I've seen good families messed up because of this stupidity.

Every time we do this, most of the audience of convicted drunks put on their poker faces—or maybe their bar faces—and pretend they aren't listening and that those stories don't affect them. But they do. And they listen, and sometimes a tear rolls down their faces, or they look down at their feet, staring into their souls.

When I get home, I'm not fit to be around, and I try to hide in a book or the newspaper. But I'm not really there. I'm looking into my own soul, too, and wondering about the insanity of it all.

Alcohol is a big part of my community. Our county is usually in the top two or three counties in the state for alcohol purchases per capita. Oh, we're a tourist area, but still, we more than hold our own. Some folks say we're a logging and fishing community, and that's true, though not as much anymore. Some blame the weather; and yes, we do live in a rain forest, and the winters can be pretty bleak and isolating, if not downright depressing.

We as a community still drink a lot, and this is part of our culture. All the lodges around here have bars, and the big charity events are well lubricated with alcohol.

Kids see that and are part of it. There are a lot of keggers up in the woods and at the beach, and there are a lot of private parties too. Often the parents are the ones who do the beer run and buy the kegs.

Twelve percent of our fifth-graders say they've drunk alcohol, and half of them have gotten drunk. One-fourth of our eighth-graders say the same thing.

When that survey was published in the weekly paper, it made headlines, but only one person wrote a letter to the editor about it. I was fired up enough about it that I wrote an op-ed piece about it, but no one followed up with a letter the next week.

Some folks liked what I said. A grocery clerk and a barber told me I was right on the money and that it was an enormous crisis. A few other people said they'd heard me loud and clear. But they weren't going to say much out in the community, because, well, you know, it's just what we do around here.

My Op-Ed Piece

There is an ill wind blowing through our town. It steals our hope and the childhood and energy of our kids, and it steals our strength to build our families and our future. It takes our jobs, and it takes food from the mouths of our children. It leaves us sick and frail, too weak to care for ourselves and the people we love.

We don't talk about this toxic wind in the room, and we quickly sidestep the difficult questions it raises as we go about our lives and step around the corpses of its victims.

If this ill wind was the Black Death or an oil spill on our beaches or another Tillamook Burn (a series of massive forest fires from 1933 to 1951, burning and re-burning over 550 square miles of old growth forest), we would rise up in the streets and fight this disaster head-on, with all our collective energies and resources.

But we don't. Once in a while, after one of our youth is killed in an alcohol-soaked crash, or there is a serious assault or homicide caused by booze, we wring our hands and bemoan the prevalence and power of alcohol abuse in our town. But a few weeks later, the topic of conversation changes, and we go on.

Over three hundred people are arrested in our county each year for DUIs, and yet people still refer to this crime as "getting a ticket," and say, "Well, it's just a DUI."

Yet this wind blows deeper and deadlier into the heart of our community. Our grade-school kids tell us that 12 percent of them have been drunk at a party, 37 percent started drinking when they were nine or ten years old, and half have ridden in a car driven by a drunk. Four percent of these kids report they've been too hungover to make it to school.

The numbers get worse in junior high: 14 percent drink on a weekly basis, 23 percent binge drink (more than five drinks), and 8 percent binge drink monthly. Eighty-five percent think drinking and driving is a serious community problem.

High school kids: By age fourteen, 44 percent have used alcohol, 12 percent have driven drunk themselves, and 19 percent of our kids have been injured when they are drinking.

The numbers go on and on, and we could all point fingers or wring our hands at these tragic numbers.

Or we could applaud and cheer, as so many of us did at this year's high school graduation, where the student speaker was bragging about her "graduation MIP" (a traffic ticket for being a minor in possession of alcohol) as a rite of passage, and a large part of the audience responded with applause and cheers. I was there, and I wept for my town.

Every day I see the faces and the wreckage of underage drinking and the personal costs of our society's acceptance of alcohol abuse. I see kids dropping out of school, not applying themselves to build healthy families, find productive work, or raise their own kids. I see their bruises and their already-long driving and criminal records.

I see their young faces as they walk the chain gang through the courthouse on the way to criminal court and more jail time. I read their names on the jail roster every morning. And with some of them, I see their meth sores and heroin needle marks. But all of those kids tell me the problem started with booze.

Kids tell me all time about their loss of hope, the emptiness of their family lives, their yearning to find a safe place to be with their friends, and their hunger for a meaningful, productive life. Our kids in trouble have good values, and they want to succeed. They need our help to beat this ill wind and put this storm to rest.

I'm a believer in the rule of law and the law as a statement of our community values and dreams. I'd better believe that. You have entrusted me to be a judge and to be fair and apply justice. Yet as I go about my work to enforce the law and change behavior, I am often left at the end of a day on the bench, feeling like the Dutch boy holding his finger in the dike. I listen for an alarm bell.

Yet there is a great silence. After last June's flurry of articles and discussion about that graduation speech, the public clamor died down. Since then more people have died, more people have been assaulted, more people have driven drunk, more people have gone to jail, and more kids have started drinking. We are left with a nasty wind whipping through our town, and we need to bind our wounds and set a new course for how we live and how our children are raised.

Our community is rich in resources. We have great health care providers, counselors, and self-help groups, and there are nightly meetings of people in recovery. Yes, we've come a long way since I was a kid myself in this town. I've seen some good changes. But we need more.

It is time, my neighbors, for all of us to rise up and to be angry about this ill wind, and to find horror in the message we are getting from our young people. Our kids see alcohol abuse as a very serious problem. It is time that we listen to what our kids are saying. It is time to be mentors, to be activists, to calm the storm.

It is time to be outraged. It is time to talk about the elephant in our town's living room.

(Neal Lemery, "An Ill Wind is Blowing", *Headlight Herald* [Tillamook, OR], October 8, 2008.)

That survey and my words in the paper still echo around the community, and I hear those numbers and that concern on a lot of lips.

Terry

Terry came to court with a driving-while-suspended and a careless-driving ticket. He was angry at himself and angry at the world. His family life was in turmoil, and his family had insisted that he get some counseling. Looking at his driving record and listening to him rant for ten minutes, I could only agree.

There was a big storm raging in this young man, and he was frustrated with trying to figure out how to sail through the storm and find a safe port. He didn't really want to get washed overboard, but he used his anger and behavior to keep everyone a safe distance away.

I wrote to him after court, hoping that a letter in his mailbox a few days after court—yet another battle in his life—would find a quiet ear and an opportunity to do some reflection. I wanted him to feel that I'd taken off my robe and put my sword of justice and vengeance back in its sheath. He'd spilled enough blood of his own in his struggles.

Dear Terry,

Of greater importance (other than your legal issues) are your well-being and your sobriety.

Life is a journey, and as with any project or trip, we men often find that we don't always have the right tool or enough nails for the project. As we are in charge of our life journeys, it is OK to stop to get more tools, rest, and even change direction. All in all, we need to know what tools we need, to get the right map, to plan ahead, and to move in the direction we want to go.

Sobriety is a spiritual crisis. The Chinese character for "crisis" is a combination of danger and opportunity. When we are in crisis, it is the universe giving us the signal that it's OK to change direction.

Sobriety is one day at a time.

Sobriety is working the Twelve Steps.

Sobriety is assembling the Terry Team and calling on other team members for support when support is needed. Go, Terry! The team is always available. The team is always ready.

The team does not judge but instead is supportive and firm. The team won't put up with bullshit and insincerity. The team will spot deception and destructive thinking and will ask Terry to get back on track. Terry knows this and relies on himself and the team for support, consistency, and respect.

Forgiveness. Oh, you struggled with that this morning. It is a struggle, and it's hard. Self-forgiveness is especially hard, because both you and I have had those powerful people and voices in our lives convince us that we are worthless and powerless and that we need to fail in our lives, as that is our destiny. Oh, those voices and people are *so wrong*!

I choose not to play their games anymore and not to listen to them anymore. Instead, each day I choose to love myself, to feel God's love inside of me, and to share that love with others in my life. Part of that self-love is forgiveness.

Forgiveness is not forgetting. Forgiveness is recognition and understanding of the wrong and the bad influences. Given that knowledge, I can then choose to learn from those experiences, to develop an understanding of those people and words and the influence they have had on me in my life. Then I move on under my own power and make my own way in the world. I choose not to empower those voices and those people anymore.

Forgiveness makes those people and those voices impotent in my life. I cut off their power over me. Then I can focus on the light in my life and enhance the good things in my life. I surround myself with good people and with good thoughts.

I talk to myself a lot and tell myself that I love myself, that I am worthy of love, and that I am an instrument of God's love in this world. Part of that love is loving myself. Part of that love is loving you.

Once a week I have coffee with my good friends, and we talk about our lives and our spirituality and what sacred and wondrous things have occurred in our lives in the past week. We also talk about our challenges and our spiritual struggles. We pray. We hug. It's a vital part of my life.

Every morning I have coffee with my wife. Sometimes we talk about important stuff, and sometimes we talk about "unimportant" stuff. But we connect, and we communicate. She is my best friend. It's all about relationship and taking time for the relationship.

You are an example for your brother. He is hungry for a father and a brother who can help him now. He is hungry for a relationship and for meaning. I too have been the visiting father figure for youth in prison; and I too have had to pull over on the side of the highway after a visit and have a good cry.

Yet that was a productive time for one of my young men. He developed some self-esteem, he had access to great counseling, he had support from foster parents, and he was safe from a horrific home environment. He gained perspective. He was able to rest from his struggles and rearm himself to deal with the struggles of life. It was a time to "retool."

Prison time can be a fertile time. Your brother needs to hear about your journey. He needs your support. He needs your example.

Keep a journal. Write down your thoughts, your hopes, and your fears. Sometimes go back and read what you have written. You will find insight and direction. You will find meaning. You will be impressed with your wisdom and insight.

Write to your brother. Put some of your thoughts and advice down on paper so he can refer to it and be inspired. He will know you care. He will know you are there for him. In return, you will be rewarded and enriched.

I think you need a counselor, with whom you can dig into your own heart and pull out the pain and anger inside of you. Find the source of your wounds and then drain out the pus and cleanse yourself. Let the healing begin. We all need that objective person in our lives who is detached enough from the daily crap and garbage and personalities—someone who can give us a fresh look. We need someone who can ask us the tough questions and demand that we find the answers. (I was a bit of that with you this morning, and you had to deal with a lot of your pain. And it was good.)

Healing takes time, so be patient. Reward yourself for your work by doing your snowboarding and your other hobbies and sports. Reward yourself by finding beauty in life. Reward yourself by telling yourself you love yourself every day.

Get an education. Get an education. Get an education. It's a gift for yourself that no one can ever take away from you. It will enrich your life beyond money and a better job. It will enrich your relationship with your girlfriend. You are also a role model for your brother. Show him the value of education.

Keep in touch. Write to me. If you come over here, I'll buy you lunch. I'm part of the Terry Team.

When you are working with your counselor and you reach a wall and you need some help getting some really tough stuff out on the table, I can be there for you and cheer you on. I know where you live, and I can give you a hug again.

You are worthy. You are loved. Others see that in you. Now it is time for you to see that in yourself. So do this important work. Don't start tomorrow. Start today.

I never heard back from Terry. I'm not sure I expected to. But I still wrote that letter.

Mentoring is like that. You do your work; you invest some time and some energy. You put in a lot of compassion and respect. You don't do it for the idea of a reward in the form of a mushy thank-you card or a return visit with a big hug and flowers. If that is what you need to be mentoring someone, you are in the wrong business.

Mentoring is meant to be selfless; it means being a giver and not a receiver. Mentoring is an act of giving, a giving deep inside of yourself— a giving of your heart. It is the act of giving that is the reward.

The mentor is the Johnny Appleseed of human relations. Go plant the seeds, but don't expect to be invited to the harvest. Oh, there will be harvests, and you will be blessed. But the real blessings come when you don't expect results.

twenty-five

Family: It's More than the Dictionary Definition

What is family? They were the people who claimed you. In good, in bad, in parts or in whole, they were the ones who showed up, who stayed in there, regardless. It wasn't just about blood relations or shared chromosomes, but something wider, bigger. We had many families over time. Our family of origin, the family we created, and the groups you moved through while all of this was happening: friends, lovers, sometimes even strangers. None of them perfect, and we couldn't expect them to be. You can't make any one person your world. The trick was to take what each could give you and build your world from it.
— *Sarah Dessen, Lock and Key*

"How's your family?" someone asked the other day.

"Oh, fine," I replied. The standard response.

"No, really. How are they?" the person asked again, wanting me to be honest, to engage with him.

I shared some successes and a few challenges, feeling myself break into a smile as I talked about the people I loved, people I shared my life with, people who really mattered to me.

The conversation got into how I was really doing at this point in my life—how I'm really close to retirement and busy with my music, my mentoring, and the usual busy schedule of late summer.

It felt good to connect with that person and to have someone really care about me—where I was in life and how things were really going. It was one of those times when I was glad I lived in a small town, where you could run into people who really cared about you, who were good friends. I felt that warm, deep feeling inside me: that feeling that people really cared about me, that I mattered, that what I did in my life really mattered.

As I walked down the street, I wondered, Well, what do I mean when I mention my family?

My lawyer brain first thinks of the dictionary definition of *family*. I look back at those in my life I'm related to biologically. Except for a few, they aren't family now. We don't have anything in common except some DNA and some quirky personalities and mannerisms. Some of them share a last name with me. But all that doesn't add up to family for me. Not anymore.

I ran down the list of names, the names of my family, their faces popping into my head, more warm feelings filling my chest and my gut, being part of the smile across my face.

It struck me hard that those I feel are family aren't related to me by blood. We don't share the DNA or any of the quirky family traits of personality, habit, or behavior. We don't share last names or common ancestors.

No, my family doesn't fit the Webster's definition. But they are my family.

They've come into my life through my marriage, my work, my life in this community. Some of them have lived in my house and sat with me at the dinner table as I watched them grow up and move on, making something out of themselves.

Some of them are people I just see a lot, who share some laughs, tell stories, and have fun and good times. They are the people you don't need to worry about when you see them, worrying about what you will talk about or what you will do. Like your favorite pair of worn jeans, they fit right, and they're comfortable without any effort, without any work about being formal or proper or even polite.

They know who they are with me: family. When I try to explain to someone else how they are related to me, how they are family, the usual words of *relationship* and *kinship* just don't work.

"Stepson," "former foster son," "mentee," "former coworker," "wife's former stepdaughter," and whatever I might use to "define" our relationship are just a group of words. They don't work very well. They don't describe who we are or how we are related. All those words aren't what we are to each other anyway.

Some of the phrases have become nonsense to me. How can one be a "former" son? Once one, always one. English needs to develop some new words for who's who in my family.

We've had a lot of shared experiences: a lot of fun, a lot of struggle sometimes, a lot of water under the bridge. More wrinkles, maybe less hair, bigger stomachs—all marks of aging. We all have a bit more gray in our hair—some, including me, a lot more than others!

If we all got together for a family portrait, you wouldn't be able to tell we're related by looking at our faces, at how we dress, how we smile, or how we sing. But you would know us by our stories, by our affection for each other, by our shared experiences, and by our love for what we really are to each other. You would know us by that love that is deep in our hearts—the love we have for each other that no one can define.

In all that we are family.

twenty-six

Kana Hanai, the Adopted Child

Sherman made the terrible discovery that men make about their fathers sooner or
later... that the man before him was not an aging father but a boy, a boy much like
himself, a boy who grew up and had a child of his own and, as best he could, out
of a sense of duty and, perhaps love, adopted a role called Being a Father so that
his child would have something mythical and infinitely important: a Protector,
who would keep a lid on all the chaotic and catastrophic possibilities of life.
— Tom Wolfe, The Bonfire of the Vanities

The Hawaiian words *kana hanai* (ha-NI) are loosely translated as "my adopted child or children" or "my foster child."

It is the taking in of a youth who needs some parenting, some nurturance and love; it is different from the love and nurturance of biological parents. The *hanai* child becomes part of the family not only physically but also emotionally. That child is treated as one of the family's children; he or she is loved and nurtured and cared for as one of their own. You become an "extra" parent, the additional aunt or uncle. There's a lot of aloha --- unconditional, unlimited love and concern.

When I was growing up, *hanai* children could occasionally be found at our dinner table or could spend a month with us in the summer. My mother spoke lovingly of her aunt and her ninth year of life, when she lived with her aunt and uncle and saw the world in a different way, soaking up her aunt and uncle's love and concern. That year got my mom through some tough times and gave her new strength and a new lease on childhood.

In our house there was always an extra chair and room at the table for another face. If we had dessert, we all shared. None of us kids dared to complain. Having another kid at the table was nothing new, and Mom would always be a little happier than usual as she was cooking dinner. Conversation around the table was always lively and included the child, making him or her feel welcome and part of our family.

My wife and I carried on that tradition of welcoming kids into our home after we got married and took it further. We lived in town, and my stepson's friends were usually in the yard or playing music in the house. When it was dinnertime, we set the table with another plate or two and shared our food and conversation. There was always laughter and some good stories.

Sometimes when we would plan a family outing—a picnic or a hike—that other kid who seemed to be in the house a lot usually came along.

A few years after my stepson went to college, my wife came home from school one day with a sad story, telling me about one of her students who needed a place to live. Another son, she said—a *hanai* child—needed to come home. He would be our *hana hanai*.

The spare bedroom became his room. I found an old dresser for ten dollars, sanded it down, and put on a couple of coats of paint. Our dinner table was now set for three, and we had teenage music and laughter and mood swings in our house again. We had a front-row seat to watch this newest man-child grow up and find his passions.

Soon his friends would come by and manage to stay for dinner and breakfast. When they were busy having fun downstairs and watching a movie or playing games or listening to music, I'd knock on the door with a plate of cookies fresh out of the oven and a jug of milk.

There were looks of amazement and big grins as the plate of cookies and the milk quickly disappeared.

We'd take some of those kids to the beach, along with our dog, and pack extra food in the picnic basket.

One summer one of the boys had pretty much moved in, and I was wondering whether I needed to remodel the storage room into his bedroom. About a week later, his mother called. The guy had been sleeping on our couch, and the end of the kitchen table was his regular place at dinner.

"Is Joe there?" she asked.

Indeed, he is, I thought. *And it took you over a week to realize you hadn't heard from him?*

Oh, Mom, you've missed a week of his laughter, of his giggling when he plays fetch with the dog down on the beach. A week of his jokes at the dinner table.

No wonder he's about moved in here. We've been keeping track of him, making sure he has a few meals every day and a place to sleep. His laundry gets washed, and he's taken on a chore or two to do around here. It's all part of being in the spirit of *hanai*.

One time we took these *hanai* boys to the big city with us on our annual August back-to-school shopping trip. I'd had to make a quick trip down the road, about forty miles, one night to help one of them get his back-to-school money from his dad before his dad headed off to the tavern with that cash in his wallet.

There was real fear in the eyes of this *hanai* child—fear that the money would be drunk up before we got there that night. On the way back home, he fell asleep in the back seat of the car, worn out from a day of worrying, his school-clothes money safe in his wallet.

When we hit the big stores in the city, my newest *hanai* child grinned as he was buying his school supplies. He cried when I had him pick out a new backpack and put it in my cart.

"For you," I said. "You need a new one for school, you know."

He looked away, leaning on the shoulder of our foster son, tears welling in his eyes.

Kids grow up, and they move away. I never feel really bad when I wave at them as they head off. It is time for them to go; their wings are strong, and they are ready to fly. We've done a good job, being good parents to each one of the *kana hanai* who have come into our lives.

We still have our *kana hanai*. Most of the newer guys live not too far away—behind prison bars. They stumbled and fell when they were kids and are working on reinventing themselves, learning to become adults. There are a lot of reasons for that, but they're still just kids, young men wanting to test their wings, wanting to be part of normal. We go see them often, and we celebrate their birthdays, listen to their stories, and ask how they are doing in school, how they are making their way through their lives.

We pay attention to them, we care about them, and we listen to them. We show up, and we come to visit when we say we are coming. A lot of that is foreign to them, and they don't know quite what to make of it. Just like a lot of the other *hanai* kids I've had in my life, they are kids who just want to be normal.

When they get out of prison, they come to our house, eat dinner with us, play games, and go to the beach. Just like all the other *hanai* children in our lives, we put their pictures on the fireplace mantel and talk about them with our friends.

We visit them and spoil them as they share their challenges and their successes with us.

A few years ago, we spent some time in Hawaii, talking with families and some parents of *kana hanai*. We shared our stories and our love for our adopted ones, lost kids we opened the door to and invited in for some family time, providing a refuge from the world and a place to laugh and be themselves.

In Hawaii those who have *hanai* children have a special place in the community. They have a special place in the village—a place of honor and respect. They are seen as the special glue that keeps their culture healthy and their children strong. *Kana hanai* families are a big part of the fabric of the community. They are saviors of youth who could become lost and even be thrown away.

My village isn't in Hawaii, but we have a lot of *kana hanai* and a lot of parents of their beloved *hanai*. Together we are raising a stronger village, rich in kids and rich in the spirit of aloha and *kana hanai*.

I wouldn't have it any other way.

twenty-seven

Figuring Out Father's Day

Listen, there is no way any true man is going to let children live around him in his home and not discipline and teach, fight and mold them until they know all he knows. His goal is to make them better than he is. Being their friend is a distant second to this.

— *Victor Devlin*

I walk past the large display of Father's Day cards in the store, not stopping to browse to find the perfect card to send to a father. A twinge of sadness stings my gut, bringing back that old feeling: a mixture of grief, loss, and an emptiness that can't be filled.

The greeting card companies and the TV ads tell me I'm supposed to make Father's Day a special day for my dad. But they're missing the point, and they sure don't understand my life and how I think about Father's Day.

Dad has been gone for most of my life. And even when he was around and I got him a card, he'd just nod, barely saying the "thank you" I'd been craving. My stepdad has been gone a long time, too. I knew he liked my cards. He'd smile and give me a hearty handshake. We knew where we stood with each other. We just didn't say anything. Talking about love and fathering wasn't part of our conversations. But we knew. That was enough for me.

My father-in-law liked my cards, too. He'd chuckle and laugh, and there'd be a twinkle in his eye. He got a lot of attention on Father's Day, and he knew he was loved. He gave it back, too—in spades.

This is my second year without him, and the emptiness inside me as I look at all the choices on the card rack feels a bit deeper.

I'm on the other side of the coin now. I have a bunch of sons. My stepson and I are close, even though he's about six hundred miles away. We can share our love easily, with just a smile, a joke, or something funny we e-mail to each other. We still joke with each other, and we still play pranks on each other with a silly plastic lobster. A few weeks ago I found Mr. Lobster again, and he starred in my movie, the one I made on my iPad and sent to my forty-two-year-old son.

A few hours later, my son sent me an e-mail. He was in hysterics over my three-minute movie and invited me to share it with the rest of the family. I wasn't sure he thought I would, but I did—showing him that I, too, could make my way around YouTube and make some jokes again with Mr. Lobster.

One of my foster sons flies his paraglider way up in the air, sending me videos once in a while of him looking down at the faraway ground or a jetliner flying underneath him. He knows I'm scared of heights, and I worry about him jumping off cliffs, flying high in the air, turning somersaults, and making loops. I know he's laughing every time he sends me his latest aerial adventures. It's his way of saying he loves me and that he's doing just fine.

I have other sons now, too: the young guys I mentor in prison and some of the other guys there. The young man who makes the coffee drinks at the prison canteen on visiting days knows my usual order, and he gets it started the moment I walk in the door. Other guys show me their artwork or tell me about doing well on a test or moving ahead in their treatment. I get a lot of "Hi, Neal"s when I show up on their special days or sit in on one of their activities, being a dad in their lives.

Their own dads don't show up much, if at all. So I like to give them a smile and a handshake just to say hi, just to say they are important.

I don't find the "sons" section among the Father's Day cards. There are the golfing-joke ones, the religious ones, the silly ones, even the stepdad ones now. But there aren't any cards that say what I want to say: "Good job, Son. Thanks for being the son. Without the son, there'd be no Father's Day. I'm proud of who you are, and what you've become."

That's what this day is really about: sons and daughters. The dad takes on the job of helping to raise the child: to teach, to listen, to wipe snotty noses and change dirty diapers, and to help them with their homework. He listens and counsels, and he shows them by example how it is to be a man, to move along in the world, to be healthy and wise.

I don't have daughters, but I know they're watching their dads too.

"How are you at this man stuff? How do I live with you? What kind of man do I want in my life? While you are at it, teach me about trust," they say.

It is the biggest job I've ever had. There's a lot of teaching of respect and capability, and a lot of unconditional love.

We're supposed to show them what love is all about, along with respect, compassion, and learning about this crazy world.

Being a dad is really learning how to be a good example to be watched and judged.

"How *are* you doing as a man? Show me. But I expect you to do it right."

No pressure there!

By the way, the manual on all this stuff is out of print, and I can't find an old copy on Amazon.com.

We're the guys who wait by the door at night, making sure they get home safe from that party or that big date. We're there to listen, to nod, to simply be there, to keep the porch light burning—to be the guy who cares that they do have a home to come back to after a day of being a teenager in a harsh, often indifferent, and cruel world.

We give the hugs, wipe the tears, and look them in the eye, quietly telling them we believe in them. All things are possible. They are loved.

Such simple things we do. But when that simple stuff gets neglected or no guy is behind the front door when they do come home late at night, then all hell can break loose. Their fragile ships at sea too often crash onto the reefs and sink in the storms.

We're the guys who haul the laundry sack to the laundry room when they come home for the weekend. We fire up the barbecue and cook their favorite foods, letting them hang out with their old friends. We often take a backseat then, letting them visit and laugh with their friends as we flip the burgers and get more potato salad out of the fridge.

There will come the time when they'll sit down with us on the couch after the party and after a long day at the beach with their friends. Then they'll talk, a bit shy at first, then go deep, talking about the serious questions of life a young man has once he gets out in the world and has to deal with all of life's adult problems and worries.

Then we listen, and we listen hard. Sometimes they ask for advice, but mainly they just want to talk, to show you they are doing OK, that they learned a lot from you about life, and that they are doing pretty well at it.

We let them know—right back at them—that they're doing a good job and that we believe in them and take pride in whom they are becoming.

It's pretty easy to sit there and listen, to nod, and to say a few words of encouragement.

You see, fatherhood is a whole bunch of just showing up, just being present in someone's life.

You don't need to give them your DNA, but you do need to give them your time and your love. That's fatherhood. That's being a real man.

The good work comes in answering the phone or texting something sweet back in the middle of the night, letting them know you are around and that you care.

I get my thanks, then, for being the dad. I get that when they don't call for a couple of weeks at a time. I know they are fine: they are making their way, needing their independence, flexing their big-boy muscles, and making their way through life.

Someday, Hallmark might figure it out and start selling "I love my kids" cards for Father's Day. But until they do, I'll just keep on doing what I do best: loving all my kids with all my heart and telling them every chance I get that I love them.

That's what dads do.

twenty-eight

Being Grandpa: Two Generations Apart

You have to do your own growing no matter how tall your grandfather was.
— *Abraham Lincoln*

My grandson is a teenager, struggling with high school and a social life, and having his share of anger and questions about the real world and where he is going.

I wrote to him one day, worried about giving a young man some direction and grandfatherly advice, hoping he'd listen just a bit and make some good decisions in life.

Mentoring a young relative is harder. The stakes are higher, and there's love and family dynamics that make the relationship a lot more complicated. Still, a grandfather really is a mentor for a grandchild. It is probably one of the most important mentoring jobs one could ever find.

> Dear Nathan,
>
> In my work I often find myself giving some advice to young men who are finding life a challenge and who seem to be a bit lost.
>
> I am enclosing a letter I just wrote to two young men, whom I hope to have pointed in the direction of going to college and getting out of the dead-end jobs, drugs, and alcoholic lifestyle they have fallen into.

As you begin high school, you are now in that age-group in which people are making those kinds of decisions. By not deciding, by not being proactive and self-caring, they then accept the low road and don't aspire to anything of value.

So I'm sharing this advice with you. Granted, it's stuff we all know, but it's good to review it and be reminded of our call to a higher level of existence. We all have choices. Every day there are choices. Life is an attitude as much as anything else.

So choose your attitude.

Also, choose something hard. Something in life will always be hard. But working on something hard is life's biggest challenge and also its biggest reward. Getting a "hard" done is a great accomplishment and proves your mettle as a man. So choose well what is your "hard."

You know that I expect good things from you this year in school. You are in your last "free" school. There are great teachers at your high school, and there are great students. You have rich opportunities. Your task is to find those teachers and students and to obtain their gifts for you. It's a treasure hunt.

Or you can choose not to seek out challenges and not to seek out excellence in teaching and in your peers. You could settle for mediocrity. You could settle for mere existence.

But is that being true to yourself? Is that honoring your dreams? Is that showing respect for yourself?

The Army has a great slogan: "Be All You Can Be."

This is all truly up to you. You have resources: your brains, your health, your youthful energy, your enthusiasm, your family, your friends, and your school. Your job is to master all these resources and get the work done.

The luxury here, at this time in your life, is that you have a lot of freedom to choose what you want to get out of high school. You can coast by, or you can drop out. Or you can challenge yourself and "find your hard." Then do your "hard" and get some accomplishments under your belt.

This is not about getting good grades. It's not about floating by or taking it easy. Life in general is hard and has its challenges. How you deal with the hardness and the challenges is the measure of your manhood. Anyone can coast and slack off and get by. There is no honor in that.

Some people will measure your performance by your report card. I don't. I would measure your performance by asking you whether you lived and worked to your potential in a class. A grade is simply one way to rate performance, but it's not always accurate. In some of the best classes I had, I received Bs, Cs, and Ds.

One year in high school, I got an F in PE. I got the F simply because I was a fat kid and didn't do as many push-ups, sit-ups, and pull-ups as other kids. I ran last in the mile. But for myself, I got an A. I lost weight, I improved my ability to do exercises, and I got better in the sports we played. So I felt successful, and I "worked my hard." I didn't let the grade get me down. I knew in my heart what I had done there. I moved on. Lesson learned. Not a failure. It was my choice.

I don't buy your excuse that "I'm not my sister." That is simply a BS excuse. Of course you are not your sister. Truly professional educators and intelligent people won't compare you to your sister. Instead, compare your work to *your* standards of excellence. That is the true measure here of your performance. So don't BS yourself. You deserve more honesty than that and more integrity.

I expect the best of you. I expect that because I know you well enough to know what you are capable of and that your "best" is truly awesome.

I'm your grandfather and your friend. I'm always in your camp and always on your team. If you get stressed out or bewildered or just need to talk, then pick up the phone and talk to me. If you need to do that in person, I'll come to you.

This is an exciting and challenging time in your life. You are on a steady course, and you have under your belt an impressive record of performance, knowledge, and skills. It's time to build on all that and walk down that "high road"—the road to achieving your dreams.

No one expects you to know "what I will do with the rest of my life." Those opportunities, those challenges, and those choices will come in due time. For now you need to get ready to meet those challenges and to make those decisions by further developing yourself and honing your skills and wisdom.

You see yourself as a warrior. So be the warrior.

You don't win the cross-country race by first putting on a pair of running shoes that morning. You train. You do the physical training and the mental training. You do it over time. The good work—the "hard" work in anything—is also like that. You train. You educate yourself, you do your homework, and you practice. You develop skills. You believe in yourself, and then you will be ready for the race. The best runner is not always the runner who crosses the finish line first.

So no slacking this year, OK? As Larry the Cable Guy says, "Git 'er done!"

Love,
Neal

twenty-nine

Moving into Marriage

Love one another,

but not make a bond of love.

Let it rather be a moving sea

between the shores of your souls.

Fill each other's cup

but drink not from the same cup.

Sing and dance together and be joyous,

but let each of you be alone.

Though they quiver with the same music

give your hearts,

but not into each other's keeping

for only the hand of life

can contain your hearts

and stand together

yet not too near each other

for the pillars of the temple stand apart

and the oak tree and the cypress

grow not in each other's shadow.

—Kahlil Gibran, The Prophet

Jack

Jack's been a good friend of mine for a long time. We've wrestled with life's big issues in a small town and with his struggle to find the right path in college and where he wants to go after college.

He spent time overseas, engaged in demanding social services and growing into his full potential. Then he came back, hungry for a more concrete purpose in life, wondering where he wanted to go.

We talked about law school and love and living one's dreams. After one long lunch, when he anguished about his choices and dilemmas, I wrote him a letter.

Hi, Jack

OK, you motivated me to write.

There's a great song where the lyrics start out, "If I were a carpenter and you were a lady, would you marry me anyway?"

It is not one's professional position in life, or title, that really matters. It is how you live your life and how you contribute to others, and how you contribute to yourself.

What is good for Jack now? I'm enclosing my "visual" on my philosophy of life. It's a balance, and it's about finding your center. It is taking care of yourself and also honoring yourself. It is honoring your talents, honoring your skills, and honoring the hunger in your soul for what you want.

Law school wreaks havoc on love and relationships, as that world focuses on the intellectual and the abstract. The world is seen as a patchwork of analogies, logical theorems, and abstract constructs. The world becomes a place of arguments and logical progressions and the pathology of appellate court opinions.

The physical and spiritual "legs of the stool" are left to wither. That's why my interest in weight lifting and long walks took new life and also why I drank pretty heavily with my law school buddies and why our class spent most of our class funds on keggers by the river on Friday afternoons. That is why many of my classmates were divorced or broken up with their girlfriends by the time the third year rolled by.

But if one finds that balance and knows that indeed "the law is a jealous mistress," then one can do well. If I did it again, I would put my guitar and my banjo and my oil paints and my topo map of the Olympic Mountains and the Mt. Jefferson Wilderness Area and my hiking shoes in a room all their own. I would spend quite a bit of time there—as much as I spent at my desk reading those great and intriguing Supreme Court cases and writing outlines of law.

Looking back at my life, the important milestones are having good, healthy relationships and applying the tools in my tool chest to make a difference in this world.

Oh, law school gave me good and useful tools, and I've done well with those tools. But a healthy boy also has other tools in his tool chest, and sometimes those tools are the guitar and the ability to enjoy an afternoon out on the beach or along a wooded path or to scribble a few lines of a good poem that comes to him in the midst of it all.

No one is saying that not going to law school now means that that path will be padlocked and gated forevermore. If that is a path you want to walk, it will be open to you but when God and the forces of the universe deem it a good path for you. Sometimes God asks us to be patient. (See Robert Frost's "The Road Not Taken.")

You are not the typical guy. You won't be the typical law student. You have much more depth and richness in your soul than most. You have a sophisticated eye and ear, and you will get quite a bit out of law school, but you won't let it take your soul.

Ah, it is nearly a curse to be at a great restaurant where the smorgasbord spread along the buffet table has more tempting delights and pleasures than one can reasonably taste in one meal. That is, perhaps, your dilemma. You do so many things well. Being a bright man, you can do many things well, and therefore many things interest you.

Yet in life, one must also pay attention to the needs of the heart and to the finding of that special person with whom a walk through life will be an adventure and a challenge and a sheer pleasure, simply because that person is at your side during the journey.

I'm not saying that one must be the monk during law school. Yet the law is truly a jealous mistress, and when the Sunday afternoon comes when your beloved wants to walk along the river or linger over coffee and the Sunday paper or explore one's sexual appetites on a lazy afternoon, the law will call, and part of you will be drawn to reading cases on the Rule Against Perpetuities or an intriguing dissenting opinion on a contracts law case. If you are sane at that moment, part of you will wonder why you have the dilemma. But you will.

The healthy law student finds a balance and puts the mistress in her corner. One of my fellow law students worked on the green chain in a lumber mill in Albany during law school and read romance novels in French during finals week, simply to be able to say she had a life during those three years.

You are twenty-three. You have fire in your belly, and your brain is hungry. That is good. You are looking for the wild mustang to ride into your future. Yet the wise horseman doesn't always take the first horse. Instead, he waits. When the right one comes by in the corral, he knows. He wants the ride and the horse to be with him for a long time, and he wants it to be a good match.

With love, it is a rare woman who will want to walk along the path of life with such a warrior as you. Not every woman is up to the task, and not every woman will challenge and dare you to live up to your full potential.

(In a healthy relationship, you will want the woman who gets in your face at times and dares you to be all that you can be.) You won't settle for second best. But you will know her when you get to know her.

You want a woman who has her own hunger and her own journey. There will be times when you will be the cheerleader for her journey, and you will weave the reins and the rope for her when she needs to pick the right mustang out of the herd to ride with her whole heart. In that ride and in that growth, you too will grow and be happy.

In that giving of yourself, you will find your own gold.

So if there is someone who seems to intrigue you, captivate your heart, fire up your spirit, then I suggest that such a woman is rare and should not be left to wander out of your life. Perhaps it is time to get to the dance and do a bit of inquiry and negotiating and discussion.

Recently I heard a celebrity describe his thirty-year marriage as a series of great dates. I think that is right.

We all evolve during our lives. In a good relationship, we help each other grow, and we take turns throwing fresh coal on each other's embers, and we stand behind them when the wagons are circled and the enemy is shooting arrows.

Oh, perhaps there are too many metaphors in all of this, but things are rarely black and white. We deal with shades of gray, and much of life is not certain. There are few guarantees. But that keeps us sharp and keeps us at the top of our game.

As in the movie *Slumdog Millionaire*, the obvious answer is often not the right answer. The answer that is given comes from a great deal of experience.

You have great intuition. You have a great heart.

We must have lunch again, and also we need to play our guitars and sing.

Your obedient servant,
Neal

So what is marriage?

Yes, it is a partnership. It is a partnership of love, of relationship, of being housemates, of being meal mates and bathroom mates. This is a partnership that involves all twenty-four hours of the day, including the minutes before coffee and the minutes of being tired and cranky.

This is a journey. Definitely a journey. There are times when you miss the bus or come close to running out of gas or are hungry and tired or sad and lonely. Or when you need to be alone, but you are together.

Marriage is a process, an evolving animus of its own. It is dynamic and not static. But it is static in the sense of being grounded and having foundation and solidarity.

It is a refuge from the turmoil and storms in life—a shelter.

It is exhilarating and trying and soothing and solid. Sometimes all these things are going on at once.

It is someone holding your hand as you venture forth on the trail, where there are loose rocks and cliffs and thorny brush that grabs at you when you try to move forward or when you think the bear is going to eat you.

It is giving you a nudge when you are tackling something hard, and it is you nudging them as they struggle to get out of bed and out into the tough world of the day ahead.

It is your partner watching your back, and it is you watching her back.

It is growing and struggling and trying to keep it together when you really would rather stay in bed and pull the covers over your head.

It is laughing at one of the jokes you've shared for years, though no one gets the joke except the person you've shared your life with.

Marriage is knowing—without thinking—that you need to be supportive and kind and loving. It is receiving all that when you need to be supported. It is to be kind and to be loved.

It is not taking all that for granted but realizing there is treasure in all that.

It is saying that you love them, though that doesn't need to be said. But then, it actually does.

Marriage is patience, and it is keeping your mouth shut when your ego wants to fire off a comment. It is knowing when to just wait and just be there. It is being glad that your mate didn't fire off her mouth when you know what she would say. It would be true, but it wouldn't be kind or loving.

It is the oak tree and the cypress not growing in each other's shadow but growing together—supportive, independent, and dependent.

It is, as one man said to me at his wife's funeral, a continuing conversation over years and years. That, for him, was all he could hope for in life.

We are called to support people in their relationships. In that calling we are asked for our advice, our counsel. We are asked for our wisdom, and yet in our own journey, what we tell others is the very thing we ourselves need in nourishing the oak tree and the cypress as they grow with each passing year.

thirty

Dealing with Death

*I believe that imagination is stronger than knowledge. That myth is
more potent than history. That dreams are more powerful than facts.
That hope always triumphs over experience. That laughter is the only
cure for grief. And I believe that love is stronger than death.*
— Robert Fulghum, All I Really Need to Know I Learned in Kindergarten

"How do I deal with this?" a friend asked the other day as we talked
about the death of his friend at a very young age.

I don't know. I've lost friends, relatives, people I work with, neighbors, people I've admired—so many people in my life. After all that loss,
you would think I would have figured it out and known the answer to
his question.

But I don't. I explore my relationship with God, I contemplate the
universe, and I search for my place in the world: who I am, where I am
going, my own death. I sometimes think I have answers, but I also still
have questions. Big questions.

The questions nag me in the middle of the night or when I have
a thought reminding me of a loved one who has died. The other day,
when my friend asked me this question, his eyes tearing up with pain
and loss and with his quest for the answer to his question, my usual full
bag of advice and counsel didn't produce a ready answer.

Great poets, writers, artists, theologians, and my friend and I keep
coming back to the pain, the questions, the wondering.

Some say there is a plan. Yet the work of the Angel of Death seems chaotic, haphazard, completely random.

I can have a rich-yet-fleeting conversation with someone close to me, and next thing I know, I'm sobbing because he or she is suddenly gone from my life. Or I know he or she is dying, but I am still not ready for that phone call telling me his or her time has come now and not when we had thought. What I want to be rational and reasonable about is never that—not when I'm trying to understand death.

Death always screws up my plans.

I'm never ready for it—never ready for the news, the loss, the stumbling around that I do when someone close to me departs this world. I'd like to think I can manage death, but I can't. Oh, I'm practiced in helping to plan funerals and even saying comforting words and helping others out. I've mastered the legalities, and sometimes I think I know the spiritual "final answer"—but not really.

I'm not really very good at all this, and the dark void in the pit of my soul still aches, and I still cry out my laments.

Sure, I move on. I go forward. That is, after all, what we have to do in this life. I like to think part of that person's goodness and spirit lives on as a spark in my own self and that his or her love and goodness are part of the tapestry that is my life and my work in this world. Yes, all that is comforting.

Yet I still don't really know what to do or how to "handle this" to move on.

I can sit with my friend, who mourns and weeps, and let him know that there is love and kindness and compassion left in this world. I can offer that and let him take what he needs now to ease the bleeding of his own heart and his own emptiness.

Perhaps that empathy and compassion are enough. Perhaps that is the humanity I can offer as well as how we can all try to deal with death and loss and our own sense of righteous abandonment and anger.

I can live my own life well with few regrets and with passion and zeal. Then, when it is my time to leave here, those who are left behind will have seen all that in me and find some strange form of comfort in knowing I lived well and full and that love remained strong in my heart for all to see.

thirty-one

Getting Out and Moving On

There is no life—no life without its hunger;
Each restless heart beats so imperfectly;
But when you come and I am filled with wonder,
Sometimes, I think I glimpse eternity.

You raise me up, so I can stand on mountains;
You raise me up, to walk on stormy seas;
I am strong, when I am on your shoulders;
You raise me up...to more than I can be.

You raise me up...to more than I can be.

—Brendan Graham, *"You Raise Me Up"*
Music by Rolf Lovland

On the beach he found himself looking at the waves crashing onto the clean sand. Seagulls flew by and landed in a group just above the incoming tide. The skies were clearing from yesterday's storm, and the air was fresh, clean, and free.

He was alone except for the waves and the gulls and me, a hundred yards away, watching, watching over him on this first day of freedom.

I saw him gulp the cool, salty air; and then came another gulp until finally his chest relaxed, and he let it all go.

He had been released—let go from prison this morning after six and a half years. He knew the exact number of days, and he'd been counting down each one of them for as long as I'd known him.

The gate swung behind us and clanged shut. That was a familiar sound to me after all the visits here with him and other young men, but it was a new and final sound for him. Other young men had brought all his belongings from six years behind bars, filling my car, readying us for his trip today to his new life, his new beginning.

We drove away, and he could only say, "Man, oh man."

I honked the horn at the empty road ahead and offered a shouted, "Hooray!" He laughed, finally.

He fell silent after all the good-byes and handshakes and hugs with all the other young men and the prison staff. The situation was bitter-sweet after months of anticipation; he was almost afraid to go and move on with his life, going from the known and the routine into new places, new routines, and a new, fresh life.

The waves kept crashing onto the beach, and he had to run back when a wave moved up farther, almost soaking his shoes. It was a good dance, turning into a jig as he became part of the incoming tide—part of the morning at the beach, joining the world.

He'd sat down at our breakfast table, laughing at the big plate of eggs and bacon and sausage and the plate of biscuits fresh out of the oven—everything he'd ordered for this day. A real fork and a real knife—not the plastic of the last six and a half years.

I'd thought the event warranted breaking out my mother's silverware and candlesticks and china. He had placemats and all his favorites cooked to order, served on a china platter, and fresh strawberries in a dish.

I refilled his coffee and waited on him. I thought he needed that after all these years.

His birthday was tomorrow, and we had only this morning to spoil him. I'd baked him a cake, and I slipped back into the kitchen, ready for a party.

I came back into the dining room with blazing candles, and we broke out into a rousing rendition of "Happy Birthday."

He laughed and nearly cried, and he gave a lusty blow out to the candles as we applauded. I bet his wish was already granted: freedom.

He laughed again at the thought of birthday cake, and now ice cream, for breakfast. He said his grandmother wouldn't have approved, but then he laughed again and said today was probably a good reason for an exception to the rule. We laughed at his being the rule breaker, the scofflaw, not even an hour into his parole.

The sky got lighter, and he spotted the neighbor's horse in the field and the pink of the dawn. It was a new view, after all. He'd spent six and a half years in the same fenced compound, and now everything was new.

He had a second piece of cake and a bit more ice cream; then he opened up his card and his presents. Wonder sparkled in his eyes as he sat here in our house, not where we'd always visited, behind that gate—that gate that had clanged for him today for the last time. The experience was all new, and it was all delicious and sweet.

Everything was about him today—getting out and making a fresh start and moving on with his life.

Soon we'd be in the car and driving south. It was a big day. We had a lot of miles to cover and a lot of time to catch up on.

First was the beach, and then we traveled along a bay and then a river and finally through the forest. Then came farmers' fields and a city. He stared out the window, not saying much at times, and on we went.

He asked me about the trees: what they were called. And what about the salmon in the river? And what kind of logs were on that log truck?

We came to a place where we could go one way or the other. Both roads led to where we were going, so it didn't matter, and he told me which way to go. He chuckled then at the choosing of which way to go, at which road looked better. He made a decision: it was not a big deal, but then maybe it was.

In the city we met up with his good friend, a guy who had gotten out of the same place a week earlier and was doing fine. He'd settled into his new home, a halfway house. He had a 7:00 p.m. curfew, and he laughed when others there thought that was too confining. In a month he could be out until eleven. It was more freedom than he'd ever thought there could be.

I took the two young men to a steak house so they could eat their fill of meat. They'd both been craving barbecue and big, greasy ribs, and they ordered big plates of beef and chicken and a mound of fries. Using menus and ordering and making decisions on all the food were new to them, and when the attractive waitress joked around with them, they didn't quite know what to do, at least for a minute.

All too soon, the big plates were clean, and bellies were full, and smiles were seen all around.

We said good-bye to the young man we'd picked up and headed off, heading to where home had been six and a half years ago. We laughed about lunch and all he could eat and the extra slice of birthday cake I'd packed for him before we left my house.

He got quiet when the freeway sign told us how many miles it was until he reached home. All this freedom was finally getting to him—getting right into his heart.

To the side of the freeway there was a beautiful field, shining in the sun with that bright green that comes with the two or three spring-like days of February. Those days are always a tease, making us think spring is here when it isn't.

The green was real, though, and worthy of mention.

So were the sheep, grazing on the grass. There was an entire flock of ewes and their newborn lambs. The woolly babies were running and jumping, celebrating the newness of their lives and sunshine and green grass and the promise of spring.

"I'm free," he whispered then. "I'm finally free."

Fresh tears flowed then from all the eyes in the car, and we didn't speak for quite a while, caught up in that moment.

We were both free that day, even if the promised spring was not yet here. There was freedom in the air, in the rush of the incoming tide, in the color of the sky at dawn, in the light on his face from all the birthday candles, and in the dance of the lambs on the fresh, green grass of a new spring.

thirty-two

Finding My Tools in the Lost and Found

The only life worth living is the adventurous life. Of such a life the domi-
nant characteristic is that it is unafraid. It is unafraid of what other people
think…It does not adapt either its pace or its objectives to the pace and objec-
tives of its neighbors. It thinks its own thoughts, it reads its own books. It
develops its own hobbies, and it is governed by its own conscience. The herd
may graze where it pleases or stampede where it pleases, but he who lives
the adventurous life will remain unafraid when he finds himself alone.
— *Raymond B. Fosdick*

I can be so lost and alone in a crowd of people.

I plug into my electronic devices, suddenly accessing the imme-
diacy of "news," social commentary, and so many thoughts of others.
Yet I can be, at the same time, in a dark cave of despair, my isolation and
sense of unworthiness becoming the ghosts in the dark.

Friends are searching for their own meaning in life: their purpose,
their place in this hectic, frantic world of immediate deadlines and
obligations.

We heed the call of the Mad Hatter in *Alice in Wonderland*: "Hurry,
hurry."

But we can be lost, easily pushed to the side of the freeway, as the
world rushes on by.

What we have sensed we lost is being connected to each other.
We used to tell stories around the fire at night, and during the day we

worked together, laughing and singing, always connected. We shared the good and the bad.

We were close to the land, the stars, and the birds; through our hands we were connected to the earth. Our work was something we could see, touch, hold.

How we lived our day impacted our village. If we didn't hunt or plant or work together, we didn't eat. We truly connected with each other and with the universe. Spirituality wasn't abstract; it was real. We had accountability around the fire at night and around the shared meal.

Social media is popular, as we are back around the fire, telling stories, catching up, sharing our lives. But it also has its drawbacks, and we can easily be alone in a crowd, ignoring the person next to us. Nevertheless, social media life is a form of village life, of community.

Today friends write about the power of Alcoholics Anonymous, the Friends of Bill W. Why does the simple act of gathering together and sharing our lives, our fears, and our dreams work for so many people? Why does that change lives?

AA works because it is communal. It brings spirituality to the forefront of our lives. It has a belief that our spirituality and our uniqueness as a person are truly valuable and that we benefit from the spiritual energy of others. All religions, all prophets, have a core message: be connected, love one another, find peace and meaning in being in communion with each other and with the universe. Avoid separateness; don't be alone. We are all one brotherhood and sisterhood. The person next to us matters to us simply because he or she is our brother, our sister.

It is a revolutionary idea.

Yesterday I reconnected. The sun was out. It was a perfect day, almost hot and still, with the colors of autumn around me. I had plants to plant in my yard, and it felt good in my soul to push a shovel into the rich, dark soil and make a new home for shrubs, trees, and daffodils.

In sixty or seventy years, the trees I planted will reach their prime, and they will send their seeds throughout the valley and stand tall and proud, objects of beauty for those who come after me. I will be long gone, but on the day they moved here and took up residence, the trees will remember what my feet, back, and hands did for them yesterday.

Moving the dirt under my feet and between my fingers felt good. I held the plants and their roots, tenderly settling them into the ground, tucking the dirt next to their roots, and watering them in. One tree needed staking to hold it up in the coming winter storms. Yet all too soon it will be growing tall and sturdy, its roots firmly reaching downward, connecting with, and becoming part of, this land.

Being the tree planter connected me with the earth and the universe. I am part of this place, as is the tree and the hawk that circled above me and the wind that blew in from the ocean, bringing the smell of last night's rain.

Today I am far away, meeting one of my buddies and making more connections with him as he is planting his own trees and setting down his own roots. He too will grow straight and tall, his soul firmly planted in good soil, taking in the water and sunlight of knowledge and stability, making his life rich and productive.

I've been teaching him about tree planting and farming his soul. He's a good student, and what I've been saying about what we do in the village—how we are part of our tribe—is stuff he's taken to heart.

"What are you doing today?" people ask.

Making connections, planting trees, tending my soul, taking care of the brothers and sisters in this world. Finding my tools. That's what I'm doing.

thirty-three

Lighting My Candle

Everything we do is infused with the energy with which we do it. If we're frantic, life will be frantic. If we're peaceful, life will be peaceful. And so our goal in any situation becomes inner peace.
— *Marianne Williamson*

When Christmas approaches, I think about it being a time for peace and about what can make peace happen.

One would hope that peace would be on our minds every day of the year and be something we strive for in everything we do. Peace shouldn't just be one of those popular ideas of a particular season.

Many of us have religious beliefs that profess we believe in peace, that we should be peacemakers as we go about our lives raising our families, doing our jobs, and living in our communities.

Yet much of societal life is obsessed with competing, making a profit, and feeding a variety of addictions. We spend time with our technology and focus on our own lives, shunting aside the spiritual wisdom that keeps whispering, "Love your neighbors as yourselves."

If I really believe in peace and know I have a divine direction to live in peace, to practice peace, and to truly be a peacemaker, then how do I accomplish that?

I get pulled and dragged to live otherwise.

If I pay attention to popular culture and much of the media, I soon find myself absorbed by violence, bigotry, fear, anger, greed, and

141

addiction. Material possessions, instant gratification, and self-absorption fill my mind and guide my day. Yet I am left hungrier for true satisfaction, true fulfillment; and I am farther from my real purpose as a human being on this planet.

The bell ringer at the grocery store and the pile of solicitations in my mailbox tempt me to "make peace" by writing a check or putting some cash in the red kettle at the store. But does that make peace, or does it simply fuel a bureaucracy clothed in the appearance of charity and peacemaking?

Some commentators urge me to buy a bigger gun and a larger ammo clip or support arming teachers or deploying squads of sharpshooters to bring peace to the latest mass-casualty crime scene, to stop random shooting sprees, or to thwart the crazy actions of the angry sociopath who is looking for a newsworthy end to his troubled life.

The cops I've worked with spend much of their time responding to the seemingly endless calls of domestic violence, drug abuse, child neglect, and the sad loneliness in people's lives as they try to self-medicate with alcohol, drugs, and violence. Yes, the cops are peacemakers applying first aid to a troubled society we like to think is seeking peace, but so often it is trapped in the cycle of pain, violence, self-medication, and despair.

Adding more guns to that explosive mix is just creating more havoc, more violence. I suppose we would become more efficient in spilling blood and adding more fuel to the fires of anger and rage and isolation in our already self-absorbed society. I wonder what lessons we would teach our children. What would be our legacy to them?

My soul calls me to reject all that. In my time on this earth, I've seen that war and violence and anger and self-gratification don't make this world a better place. I've learned that having compassion and unconditional love and being truly selfless are the beliefs and actions that grow flowers and save souls.

I can make peace in my home, creating a place of beauty, serenity, and purpose. To truly do that, I need to make peace with myself, to truly connect with God, and to be content with my purpose in life, my real values. I need to realize that I'm beautiful and part of the universe. I need to tend to my own candlelight.

It starts with me. When I am filled with peace, then I can be a peace-maker. I can reach out into my community and be a small flame of peace and unconditional love.

Making peace isn't about writing a check or tossing some cash into a basket at a charity event. That's too easy, too simplistic. Real peace-making requires reaching out to another person and having a real conversation.

Instead, I visit the nearby prison and drink coffee and play games with young men. We play guitar and sing songs and tell stories of our lives. In our conversations I talk about my life and my struggles. I talk about love and peace. They do too. We learn from each other, and we talk about peace.

Soon those young men will be out of prison, making their way in this troubled world. The drugs, violence, sexual exploitation, and all the other war-making forces in our culture will tempt them. They will doubt themselves, and they will struggle to find their place in all that.

Yet they will have that small flame burning in their souls: the flame of self-esteem, of inner peace and universal love. They will have our relationship and their own nurtured peace-loving souls to guide and comfort them.

In their new beginnings, they will have some answers, and they will have the beginnings of a strong foundation in their lives. When they become workers and husbands and fathers, they will be on the right path, and they will know who they truly are and where they are going.

I can't change the world today. But I can start with one person and light that candle. I can nourish that small, flickering flame in the dark. That one candle lights a dark room in the depth of one's midnight despair.

With one candle, one can light the world.

thirty-four

Going Inward

Something wonderful begins to happen with the simple realization that life, like an automobile, is driven from the inside out, not the other way around. As you focus more on becoming more peaceful with where you are, rather than focusing on where you would rather be, you begin to find peace right now, in the present. Then, as you move around, try new things, and meet new people, you carry that sense of inner peace with you. It's absolutely true that, "Wherever you go, there you are."
— Richard Carlson, Don't Sweat the Small Stuff ... and it's all small stuff:
Simple Ways to Keep the Little Things from Taking Over Your Life

So, what *are* we doing here—each of us? What is it that we are doing? Just living, paying the bills, going through life day to day, not wondering what we are doing or not doing here?

The mentor ponders these questions, especially when those who seek our guidance, those who seek our wisdom, ask those questions.

How can I be wise and impart my sacred knowledge to others when I haven't even answered these questions for myself?

I keep coming back to these questions, and when I do, I have different answers, depending on where I have been, what I am doing, and where I am in my own sense of purpose—my own day-to-day relationship with God, the spirit, the universe, or whatever we want to name what seems to be beyond our comprehension. Yet being human, I want to have some order, some predictability, in my world. I want to have answers for my ever-present question of why.

The most arduous journeys are those in which one ventures inward. One can cope with the unpredictability of the airlines, crowded airports, and tight connections. One can replace the item forgotten in the suitcase or do without. When one travels, one expects to have the unexpected, the exotic, and the mind-numbing boredom of a long, tiring flight or the butt-numbing last hundred miles of a road trip.

But when I look inward, I don't have the luxury or the convenience of blaming some faceless corporate snafu, a weather-caused delay, the closed road up ahead, or the lost reservation. No, this time it's only me. If I don't face something, it's because I don't want to open that door, or I fear walking down that dark path. I don't want to deal with the monsters and the potholes I know, from past journeys there, still exist.

It's up to me to find the words, to nudge open the door, and to push open that rusty gate into the dark.

All this looking inward and wrestling with the questions of life, my self doubt, scares the bejesus out of me. Oh, I can deal pretty well with the world and all its tumult. It's a crazy place, but there are some discernible rules and practices. While the world may seem at times to be insane, my species grew up in the wilderness, and we evolved and survived in the jungles and deserts. We survived, and I've got the genes to prove it. I've made it so far. I was born of parents who survived the Great Depression and World War II. I'm a baby boomer, and I've survived nuclear bomb testing, the Cold War, the Cuban Missile Crisis, Vietnam, the Gulf War, the Iraq War, and the latest war in Afghanistan.

I've survived swine flu, bird flu, and my generation's battle with AIDS. I've even survived a heart attack and a few of the stranger family functions that have required my participation. I even survived high school, teenage acne, and teenage angst. I've even survived raising three sons and practicing law.

We humans are survivors. Survival is what we are programmed for, and our survivor skills come to the forefront because that is who we are: survivors.

When I look at my hand, I see the hand of my father, my grandfather, and my great-great-great-great-great-grandfather. It is the hand of the fifty generations before me. It will be the hand of fifty generations after me. That hand in front of my face got me here, and it's going to shape the world to get my sons and grandsons and great-great-grand-sons through life.

And who operates the hand of fifty thousand years of challenge and refinement and stamina? He's looking at me right now. That's right: me. That complex biological machine runs on genetics and intuition and brain power to be an analyzer, problem solver, and survivor. Most of the gray matter upstairs is hardwired to stay alive, put fuel in the tank, and keep on running. Hopefully there's a good amount of frontal-lobe material there that puts some thought and reason to the whole purpose of what I am doing on this earth by burning up food and consuming oxygen.

Most of us turn to religion to find the answers. We ponder the stars, the daily miracle of the movement of the sun across the sky, the march of the seasons, the length of sunlight, the migration of birds, and the cycle of life of the rest of the inhabitants of this planet. In all that searching, we grab onto a sense of order, a sense of purpose, a sense of knowing that all this struggle, all this wonder, really matters.

We all want more than just the answer of biology. Our reasoning brain seeks order, explanation, and purpose. Because most of our experiences don't seem to happen because of the mandates of Socratic logic or Newtonian physics or the hypotheses of universal order suggested by Stephen Hawking, our emotional hunger for order grabs onto the concept of God.

Oh, we give that a number of names and a number of prophets, seers, philosophers, theologians, and saviors. We as a species find in that debate for order and "being right" most of our reasons for bigotry, hatred, and warfare. We grab onto the order of "us" and "them," and we craft new words and big sets of books that set forth our stories and rules.

We want to make the universe orderly. We gaze into the starry night, and we make order by naming stars and constellations and seeing the movement of points of light as the reason we should take our rightful place at the center of the universe. And we believe God loves us the most.

Many theosophies mandate that we do all this because of faith, yet there are whispers that if all this was really logical, reasonable, and scientifically provable, we would simply believe our theology because it was true—not only because we feel it, but because it really was true.

And in all this, we are still left alone, looking up into the night-time sky, looking for God. Or we study the intricate cells of a leaf or the amazing geometry of a spider web and smugly declare that this is God's handiwork. In doing that, we still give room to the concept of mystery. For it is all a mystery.

Like the reader of a good thriller, we enjoy the chase, but we also enjoy the part where the teller of the tale puts all the clues and plotlines in order and leaves us with a nice, neatly resolved ending.

Our ancestors sat around the fire in the evening, listening to the teller of the tale about the stars, about the world, and about ourselves. We want the story to have a nice, pleasant plot and to end in time for us to head for bed at our usual time, with all the loose ends neatly tied up and everything in order. When we rise again the next day, the sun is in its place, and the village is in order, as is the world.

We live in an oral culture. Oh, we have books and papers, cities where the streets run in neat geometric patterns, and clocks that give us the reading of the minute and the hour. Our machines increasingly take away the tedium of routine chores and mechanical tasks, and our technology grows by leaps and bounds with promises of more gifts for speedy calculations.

Yet we tell stories. We love to tell stories. We love to be in the place where stories are told. Our texting and e-mailing, our addiction to instantaneous news and data, somehow comfort us, we think, by being in the know. But it is all storytelling.

We haven't really left the village. We've changed how our own village looks and who really belongs in it. It's not a matter of place anymore, but it is still our village. Our storytellers may not be sitting around our campfire, but we do have campfires and storytellers, and we keep telling our legends and our fables, and we keep celebrating our gods and the stories of our hunts and our harvests.

Yet in doing so, we have left out a few things a proper village would have and would honor as fundamental. We have let our children and our youth wander away from the fire and maybe, on a good night, find their own fire or their own storyteller. We are losing community at a time when we need to communicate more with each other and bring ourselves closer together.

The village is becoming poorer. Our children are losing their sense of purpose, their sense of being villagers in our own village. Their place at the campfire is empty and often not even recognized as a vacant seat on the log as the storyteller of the evening begins his tale.

We can see this in the growth of gangs, in kids dropping out of school, in more single-parent families and teenaged pregnancies, in the use of drugs, and in the rise of homelessness. We also see this in the eyes of young people we meet who lack a sense of purpose and a sense of hope in their lives.

All of us need a sense of place, a sense of belonging. We need a foundation on which to build our lives and shape our futures.

When that is missing in people's lives, there is a hunger, a yearning that isn't answered by consumer goods, by entertainment, or by the plethora of modern-day pleasures and culture. People want to belong, to matter, and to make a difference—to be a part of the village.

Every generation has ranted about the perceived deficiencies in the generation following them. Every society has anguished about the abilities of young people to grow up into responsible, mature, and productive citizens of the village. That is the nature of the elders: to worry about the future and lives of those who are growing up and will take over someday.

We all want purpose in our lives. When it gets right down to it, purpose means leaving an impact on this world. Our graves have headstones, and we want to be remembered. We have sons and daughters because deep down we want to perpetuate ourselves. Life is finite, so we scatter our genes and hope to reproduce ourselves. We are sexual beings because of that biological drive to be successful, to literally succeed ourselves in this world.

Yet we seem to have neglected the concept that replication is more than sexual reproduction. We also need to replicate our cultural values, our society. In generations past ancestors made sure that the culture continued, that their stories became the stories of their children, that the same songs around the campfire continued to be sung even when we didn't return from the hunt or fell dead in the fields at the end of our days.

Instead, the stories of our children aren't the stories of our own campfires, and we have left the responsibility to other forces to teach stories to our children.

We are realizing that the stories of our children aren't the stories we tell, nor are they the stories of our great-grandfathers. The stories of our village are dying out. They will die with us, and then we won't live on forever. We want that immortality. Fundamentally, we believe our God-given duty is to ensure that those stories go on and will be told forever.

Years ago I joined other men who were praying and dancing around a fire in a meadow underneath the shadow of imposing mountains. A wise man led us, blessing us with sage grass smoke, as we stripped off our modern clothing. Naked in every sense of the word, we crawled into a sacred place, a lodge made from branches and animal hides, near a fire where several men tended the coals and rolled rocks until the rocks glowed red.

In the darkness we formed a circle, our naked buttocks touching the damp earth, the only light coming from an opening in the hides through which we'd crawled. In the center, the earth was blackened by fires of past ceremonies. Another round of smudging with sage grass occurred. This is a purification, the smoke of burning sage leaves wafting around our bodies rids of us our daily worries and tasks, bringing us into Sacred Space. Then a soapstone pipe was passed. We each inhaled the sweet and bitter smoke of tobacco, and a young man began to chant softly.

Soon the door was shut, and the shaman began to pray, bringing in the ancestors and blessing us for what we were doing, for what we were becoming.

A few hot rocks were gently thrust into the lodge, finding their place in the center. The branches and hides above us were low, and we couldn't stand. The heat from the rocks and the heat of our bodies combined into a steamy sauna. The smell of sage grass, tobacco, and sweat filled my nostrils, and I fought the urge to panic and run naked back into the world.

Our leader chanted more prayers, bringing in the spirits and the Four Directions (a Native American spiritual view that Divinity is found all around us, in every aspect of the world), and this became a sacred space. I was stripped of more than my modern clothes. I sat naked before the spirits, and I became part of this holy place.

There was nothing to do but sweat and contemplate my existence, my relationship with the universe and with God. The men I was with were doing the same—all of us naked, fearful, and becoming one with Spirit. There was no place to hide.

Our ancestors were present, and it was time to face them, to be accountable, to acknowledge their wisdom and the heritage they had passed on to us.

The unspoken questions were these: What have we done with this legacy? How have we honored this trust?

The sage grass was burned again, and more hot rocks were brought in. The native herbal tobacco pipe was passed around again, and more prayers were chanted. I fell into the rhythm of the old ways, which were really my ways, the ways of life I had conveniently forgotten in my quest to be modern, to be the "civilized" man I thought was expected of me.

In the darkness and the smell of our communal sweating, I felt the sweat rolling down my chest and the beating of my heart, cleansing my skin. As the heat and steam rose off the rocks, there was connection, closeness with my forefathers—connection I had never had before.

All there was to feel was the spiritual connection that had been lost to me. Now there was ritual and form and order for what seemed now to be so natural, so human. Spirit was present, and I was connected. The beating of the drums matched the beating of my heart, and my sweat, now soaking into the earth, was as natural and as comforting as anything could be.

The prayers and chants of the shaman faded into the background as my soul flew free, unleashed from the ropes I had created in trying to be the modern man.

I was no different from my father, my grandfather, and the generations before them. Nor was I any different from my sons and my grandsons and from those who would follow them. I was of the earth and spirit, and I was alive.

There was release and connection; and in all that, peace came into my heart.

The pipe was handed to me again, and I prayed out loud for my ancestors, myself, and my children, who would follow in my footsteps. I became part of the story around the campfire, and I felt welcomed into the village—the village I had tried to run from but couldn't fully escape.

I had been called back in time to a place without time.

Slowly I returned to a place where the air in my lungs was cool. It was a place where I could wash off the sweat and the smoke from the fire and the pipe—and where the sun fell below the mountain ridge. I was alive—more alive than I'd ever been before.

It was a sacred place I would return to again and again. Oh, not in the Western linear-time sense but in the spiritual, ethereal world of spirit, of sacred time. In that place, that dimension, there was strength and unity and completion. It was a place where I could look into my own heart and see beauty, completion, and meaning.

In all the religious services, rituals, and spiritual events where I have been present, everyone there wants the same thing: a sense of spiritual connectedness and attachment. We want to be part of something bigger, and we want to be connected.

Without connection, without being part of the village—the campfire where stories are told—we are lost in the jungle, and we are being left to die of thirst in the desert as our brethren continue their journey.

My journey continues, and I yearn for the sanctuary of the campfire circle, of the wisdom of the story, of the connection I make around that circle with my fellow man, my fellow travelers on this journey.

Mentorship is all about this journey, this yearning for connection and meaning. In mentoring others, we are also nourishing ourselves and giving ourselves meaning and purpose. Mentoring is nothing new. It is part of who we are, and it is a deep part of our very nature.

Without it we are lost; we are incomplete. We are not whole. When we are not whole, our weakness leaves us vulnerable and open to the sicknesses in our society that eviscerate and emasculate us. We are no longer the warriors and elders of our tribe; we no longer protect and nourish the village.

We are no longer men.

We must take back this birthright, this heritage. We must answer the call of our ancestors to take our place in leadership, to take our place around the campfire. We must bring in our young men to sit beside us around the fire, to hear their pain, to give them space to grow into healthy men, and to share our wisdom, to share our journey.

In that we reclaim our village, and we end the diseases of disconnection, loneliness, and disharmony.

We are warriors. In this war we must protect the village. We must answer the call to be proud, to be vigilant, and to be the fathers our sons must have.

thirty-five

Self-Care

Make your own recovery the first priority in your life.
—Robin Norwood

*Every time you don't follow your inner guidance, you feel a loss
of energy, loss of power, a sense of spiritual deadness.*
—Shakti Gawain

Take your life in your own hands and what happens? A terrible thing: no one to blame.
—Erica Jong

Mentoring is hard work—no doubt about it. It consumes you, it drains you, and it can suck you dry and also revitalize you, inspire you, and thrill you.

The issues you will deal with, the emotional garbage your young man or young woman will dig through as you sit there at his or her side, will become overwhelming, daunting, to the point that you want to figuratively set the garbage dump on fire and run away.

Yet mentoring takes time, and it takes the need to reflect and be in silence with your friend, feeling his or her pain and letting the pain just be there. We humans in the twenty-first century spend a lot of time hiding the pain, keeping it locked up; and we try to escape from its reality through our drugs, alcohol, TV watching, or busyness.

Being emotionally present and being an active listener take a great deal of energy.

The topics resound through our own souls and our own attics and basements of trash and sadness and grief, the parts of our houses we don't walk into very often because they're dirty and contain the refuse of our own lives.

Mentoring stirs all that up. All the dust bunnies under our sofas and beds come out and fly around in our lives, letting us know that we, too, have unfinished work and uncaged demons to fight.

This is messy work. Scary work.

We become mentors because of the needs we have had in our lives to be loved, to be wanted, and to be listened to. We become mentors because we want to make a difference in other people's lives and to help them avoid the pain we've gone through so they will have a better life than we've had.

In my journey I've sought a balance among the physical, the mental, and the spiritual, all wrapped up in emotion. It's a three-legged stool, with emotion being the stool itself. When one leg is short, the entire stool is wobbly and threatens to topple me off, and I am left sprawling in chaos, out of balance.

Self-care is simply recognizing the stool needs to be kept in good shape, in balance, and in good repair. Self-care keeps you balanced.

By doing this, you are also mentoring—mentoring by example—by the telling of your own story, by how you live your life. It's not polished prose or a well-rehearsed speech of encouragement. You are being watched; and in the watching, mentoring is happening.

By being healthy, you are mentoring health and a healthy response to crisis and daily life. Keeping the stool in balance is mentoring—arguably the highest level of mentoring.

What about the stories you hear? The wounds, the agonies, the anger will echo inside you. Your conscious mind will analyze, process, and develop rational responses. You will solve problems. Yet when you go to sleep, your subconscious mind will kick into high gear, sorting through all the data, comparing it to your life and the other stories you have heard. Old file cabinets in your head will be opened and sorted through, the locks on the "dangerous files" will be jiggled and picked, and old nightmares will be revisited.

Things will be stirred up—and not always in an obvious, rational manner. Events in your life you haven't resolved and haven't sorted out will be thrown out on the table for you to sort through.

Seeing the fresh pain and anguish of your friend, whom you are mentoring, will "stir the pot," keeping you from the tidy housekeeping in which you pride yourself.

Tough issues and twisted conundrums will come your way.

You are a listener, and you are a guide. You are a problem solver. Some questions and issues will not be solved and will steer the guide into the darkest part of the forest. You may get lost. You may panic.

You may lose your compass.

When you get lost, the first rule is to stop and stay put. Take a breath. Look for the obvious clues as to where the right trail is. You're smarter than the average bear, and you will find your way.

It just may take some time.

You may have to ask your own guide for directions.

Mentoring, after all, can benefit everyone. Including yourself.

Sometimes the guide is the guy sitting across the table from you, the guy you're mentoring. Turn the tables and ask for his intuitive sense, his take on it. Most people do have the answers to their problems in themselves. Life isn't all that mysterious.

You have, you know, been mentoring this guy for a while, so a big chunk of your wisdom and common sense have rubbed off on him. You're training him to be a mentor too. That is the ultimate goal.

Pay it forward.

That has been your message.

So you can be mentored, and you can be guided. By one of the best. By one you've been training.

It's OK to take a break. Vacations are good for the soul and the mind. Americans take less time off than workers in any other first-world country. Mentoring is a tough job, so a break is OK. Taking a break gives perspective and offers the subconscious mind time to rummage around, looking for some guidance and some time to reorganize the file cabinets.

Don't be discouraged. You are, after all, a farmer here. You're planting seeds and tender young plants. Some seeds don't sprout, and some seeds sprout in places and at times you hadn't planned on.

That's OK. That's life.

Don't expect people to thank you. You'll get thank-yous, and you will see lives changed. You will see some amazing things and some astonishing, courageous growth. You will recognize that you've had something to do with that.

But the real astonishment will be in the growth and change that will occur—and you won't know it.

In all that is the blessing of being a mentor.

Namaste and Godspeed.

thirty-six

The Mentor's Checklist

As a mentor, you need a checklist, perhaps a job description, of the tasks you need to perform and a road map for the experiences you will have. A lot of my work was done in the courtroom. Now I do my mentoring work in a nearby prison for youth who have been convicted of sex crimes. They are often lonely, needy young men who also have amazing resilience and fortitude.

This list is a good starting point on the art of mentoring others and learning about who you are, what you value in life, and how your experiences shaped your life.

- Be a good role model. Ultimately what matters isn't what you say but how you act.
- First, do no harm. This is the corollary to the Golden Rule. You do this work to help others and nurture young souls. "If you aren't part of the solution, you are part of the problem." -- Eldridge Cleaver
- Be on time. Be accountable and professional. Just showing up in your mentees' lives is enormous. It is often a new experience for them. If you're going to be late or need to reschedule, contact them promptly and apologize. They've experienced a lifetime of people not showing up in their lives.
- Be clean and presentable. Your visit is important to them, and by taking care of yourself and being prepared, you model healthy behavior and good social skills. One of my young men scrupulously examines my choice of shirts and is sensitive to

my breath. You are a role model in this work, and you will be examined and tested.

- Coffee and food are good icebreakers and provide a social atmosphere. You are also teaching your mentee how to socialize and chat over a cup or snack. Providing the coffee and the food is also an act that models care and compassion. The prison I visit has a canteen. The menu choices—not to mention ordering, paying, and being served our selection—have offered countless lessons in real-life living and accountability.

- Don't pry. If they have a story or a bit of their history they want to share, they will let you know. A lot of people have asked them questions about this stuff as part of their job, and you may come across as yet another social worker gleaning information and pumping them for details about stuff they probably don't like talking about. If you create an atmosphere of trust and genuine positive mutual regard, you will hear stories. Your challenge then becomes to listen without overtly dropping your jaw when they share some astonishing anecdote of what they have survived.

- Share some things about your life: your adolescence, your hobbies, a funny story you heard, some pleasant event that occurred in your life. Be a teller of nice stories, stories that don't expect a response or require them to talk about their own lives. But in doing this, you are modeling social skills and developing trust. Once there is trust, you will hear their stories and dreams. You are growing men here, which is a complicated business.

- Confidentiality. Don't gossip about your mentees or their lives and respect their privacy. They probably don't have much privacy in their lives, and this time with you will develop into a time where they can truly be themselves, let their hair down, and confide in you. Confidentiality and trust are intertwined. You are developing a healthy relationship, and you are modeling that. There is gossip in prison, too, so be professional at all times when you are visiting.

- Don't preach your own version of religion and spirituality. They've had a lot of that, and you aren't there as a minister or proselyte. You will get questions about your spirituality, and

I've tried to answer those inquiries with a lot of "I" statements and a sense of continuing inquiry and journey. This area can be a rich source of good conversations.

- Be open about your obligations as a mandatory reporter of abuse. Most mentors have a legal obligation to report child abuse and elder abuse. Let your mentee know of your obligations. I think it is a good idea to spend a few minutes early on about your legal duties, coupled with what you think mentoring is and what you are there for. Your mentees are curious about that as well, and they have ideas of what they expect from you. This is a continuing conversation. We have all grown from that conversation.

- Be open to challenges and opportunities for real change. One of my mentees disclosed to me an incident of being a victim of sexual abuse. I reported this to the staff, and the next day I sat with my young man as he told his story to a supportive team of staff members. After four years of institutionalization and countless treatment and counseling sessions, he was finally able to share this burden. My role was to be nonjudgmental and supportive, and to facilitate counseling for him. He told me later that he couldn't have gone through that experience without me at his side. That report sped up his emotional growth and his successful completion of sex-offender treatment.

- I suggest that you also have a moral obligation to report suicidal thinking, depression, and other significant emotions, thinking, and plans you hear from your mentee. Make these reports openly, compassionately, and with a commitment to be emotionally supportive with your young mentee as professional staff deal with this information.

- Be seen as a resource and an advocate for your mentee's best interests. Yes, sometimes you need to be the messenger of a "not nice" incident or state of mind. So be it. There's a bit of parenting in the job of mentor, and parents need to speak loving truth. I strive to be open and up front with what I am doing and what I value.

- You will have a continuing dialogue with staff members and your mentee about your mentee's life and well-being. Make this a fruitful time and be supportive of the work that needs to be done.

- Be mindful that some things that need to be done or said can be done only by a volunteer—someone who isn't bound by a lot of rules and procedures. For example, staff can't bring gifts for one youth. You can.

- Be sensitive to their health and emotional state. If they are tired, drained, or worried about something, let them know you care and that you are aware of their condition. Be supportive and helpful. Normalize their worries and show compassion.

- Model good problem-solving skills. Tell stories of how you have experienced difficult situations and crises. Explain how you worked through them and talk about the resources you've had for such events. If I talk about a mistake I've made, that message becomes even more meaningful and productive. You are modeling your humanity, not your divinity.

- Model respect. Be courteous, kind, and compassionate not only to your mentee but also to the staff members and other people around you when you visit. Remember, it's not what you say but how you act that is the most effective message you deliver.

- Be upbeat. No matter what kind of day you've had or what you are worried about, be positive, cheerful, and supportive. You do this to give them healthy energy and to model healthy, positive living. You can use your own experience that day to be the basis for your message and how you deal with it.

- Invite your mentees to offer suggestions on how you should handle a problem. Engage them in healthy decision-making and empathic behavior. You are partners in this endeavor we call mentoring. Learn from each other. When they are teaching you, they also learn the lesson. You are creating an atmosphere of learning and mutual positive regard.

- Plan some fun activities. A birthday, holiday, or some major event in the institution is an opportunity to plan something positive, uplifting, and supportive. Then show up for that event. Be on time and behave appropriately. Such behavior is often a new event in their lives. Several of my young men had never, ever had a birthday party or presents. Throwing a simple birthday party for them turned into the highlight of their year and glad-dened my heart beyond measure.

- Mail them something regularly, such as a birthday card, a Christmas card, a postcard from a place you've visited, a copy of an interesting article you read in the paper, a funny cartoon from the comics section, or an article about one of their favorite musicians. All these things brighten their day. Sometimes writing two sentences on a note card and sending it to them does immeasurable good work.

- Find an appropriate book for them. Suggest some good reading. You might consider reading the book together at some of your meetings, an activity that helps you assess their reading and comprehension skills and makes your meetings meaningful and productive. I sometimes donate appropriate books to the institution so that all the youth can benefit from some positive and useful materials (Scrabble Dictionary, math-tutoring educational materials, appropriate young adult novels, Native American cultural materials, and so forth). We all have books on our shelves that are gathering dust, and a donation is not only good for your tax returns but also good for your heart.

- Be involved in their education and counseling work. Attend the periodic staff meetings on your mentee and ask some questions. You will often notice things or hear concerns your mentee doesn't express to staff. When appropriate, bring those up. One of my young men couldn't see well and needed to have an eye exam. No one else noticed this, but I did, and he now wears glasses and can do much better in school. You also establish a dialogue with staff, and you show them you can be a resource for them to use in helping your mentee.

- Look for ways to bring more of the community into the institution. Last year my wife and I arranged for a friend and his band partner to put on a concert at the institution. Everyone had a grand time, and the youth got to ask questions and enjoy a professional rock 'n' roll performance. Master gardeners and volunteers from the local Celebrate Recovery and AA organizations now come regularly, and others offer a variety of educational and cultural activities as well as mentoring.

- Respect their family time. Such time is often sporadic or even nonexistent. Be flexible and expect some emotional fallout, both before and after such events. You are part of the support system, and your mentees will naturally compare your relationship and your behavior during your visits with their family experiences. Soft-pedal the differences and don't sit in judgment on their family. Your mentees are well aware of the differences and don't need to justify or explain what they see and feel. Someday you will hear what they think. This is a good space to practice your quiet cheerleading and your skills on giving your mentee your unconditional personal regard. On the day one of my guys graduated from high school, I stepped back and didn't spend much time with him. He knew I was there, but he needed to spend time with his family. He knew I supported him, and that was enough. I still got to see him graduate, and he had the space to navigate through family waters.

- Practice self-care. Take a break once in a while. Have a "safe place" where you can process the stories you hear and the emotions you experience. You will hear some tough stories and experiences that deeply touch your heart. On the way home, there is a "crying spot" for me. Sometimes I stop there for a few minutes, and I often take some deep breaths and cry, letting the sadness, loneliness, and matter-of-fact tone of one of my guys' stories whirl around in my head and find a place to go. Yes, I carry around those stories, but I also need to process them and deal with the sadness and the tragedy of young lives. I have a big heart and broad shoulders, but I also have my limits, and I need to respect them.

- Surround yourself with supportive friends and activities so you are emotionally healthy and balanced. Then you can bring that goodness with you on your visits.

- Tell your stories of your own growth and experiences to others so these young lives can be part of your community.

thirty-seven
Quotes for Living

These quotes have inspired and guided my in my mentoring journey.

Compassion is the radicalism of our time.
—His Holiness the 14th Dalai Lama

*If you want others to be happy, practice compassion. If
you want to be happy, practice compassion.*
—His Holiness the 14th Dalai Lama

*The everyday kindness of the back roads more than makes
up for the acts of greed in the headlines.*
—Charles Kuralt, On the Road with Charles Kuralt

*The purpose of life is not to be happy. It is to be useful, to be honorable, to be com-
passionate, to have it make some difference that you have lived and lived well.*
—Ralph Waldo Emerson

*Teach this triple truth to all: A generous heart, kind speech, and a life
of service and compassion are the things which renew humanity.*
—Buddha

*The purpose of life is not to be happy. It is to be useful, to be honorable, to be com-
passionate, to have it make some difference that you have lived and lived well.*
—Ralph Waldo Emerson

Power comes from becoming change.
—Mohsid Hamid, *The Reluctant Fundamentalist*

We write to create ourselves.
—Paulann Petersen, *poet laureate emeritus of Oregon*

Treat people as if they were what they ought to be, and you help them to become what they are capable of being.
—Goethe

We make a living by what we get, but we make a life by what we give.
—Winston Churchill

If we do not initiate our sons into manhood, they will burn the village down.
—African proverb

Whatever you can do, or dream that you can do, begin it. Boldness has genius, power, and magic in it.
—Goethe

The future belongs to those who believe in the beauty of their dreams.
—Eleanor Roosevelt

A child is a person who is going to carry on what you have started. He is going to sit where you are sitting, and when you are gone, attend to those things that you think are most important. He will assume control of your cities, states, and nations. He is going to move in and take over your churches, universities, and corporations...The fate of humanity is in his hands.
—Abraham Lincoln

What lies behind us, and what lies before us are tiny matters, compared to what lies within us.
—Ralph Waldo Emerson

The greatest thing is not in so much as where we are, but in what direction we are moving.
—Oliver Wendell Holmes

It's not the load that breaks you down, it's the way you carry it.
—Lena Horne

Saying no can be the ultimate in self-care.
—Claudia Black

In the middle of difficulty lies opportunity.
—Albert Einstein

When we are really honest with ourselves we must admit our lives are all that really belong to us. So it is how we use our lives that determines the kind of men we are.
—Cesar Chavez

The life that is not examined is not worth living.
—Plato

He who knows others is wise; he who knows himself is enlightened.
—Lao-Tzu

I learn by going where I have to go.
—Theodore Roethke

Why indeed must "God" be a noun? Why not a verb... the most active and dynamic of all?
—Mary Daly, theologian

I seem to be a verb.
—Buckminster Fuller

Even when you can't win, it's best to be caught trying.
—Bill Clinton

The events in our lives happen in a sequence in time, but in their significance to ourselves, they find their own order... the continuous thread of revelation.
—Eudora Welty

The creation of something new is not accomplished by the intellect but by the play instinct acting from inner necessity. The creative mind plays with the objects it loves.
—Carl G. Jung

Every child is an artist. The problem is how to remain an artist once he grows up.
—Pablo Picasso

Nobody sees a flower—really—it is so small it takes time—we haven't time—and to see takes time, like to have a friend takes time.
—Georgia O'Keefe

Nothing has a stronger influence psychologically on their environment and especially on their children than the unlived life of the parent.
—Carl G. Jung

Go confidently in the direction of your dreams! Live the life you've imagined. As you simplify your life, the laws of the universe will be simpler.
—Henry David Thoreau

Make your own recovery the first priority in your life.
—Robin Norwood

Every time you don't follow your inner guidance, you feel a loss of energy, loss of power, a sense of spiritual deadness.
—Shakti Gawain

Take your life in your own hands and what happens? A terrible thing: no one to blame.
—Erica Jong

Stop thinking and talking about it and there is nothing you will not be able to do.
—A Zen paradigm

It is not because things are difficult that we do not dare; it is because we do not dare that they are difficult.
—Seneca

Be the change you want to see in the world.
—*Mahatma Gandhi*

We must use time creatively and forever realize the time is ripe to do something right.
—*Martin Luther King Jr.*

What we give, whether it's love, time, talent, or dollars, circulates back to us. As Scripture says, "As you sow, so shall you reap." When we sow seeds of gratitude and joy, we take a percentage of all the good that comes to us and bestow it on the universe and we harvest a life of abundance, touching and transforming every aspect of our lives
—*Rev. Mary Manin Morrissey*

One generation plants the trees, the next gets the shade.
—*Chinese proverb*

I always wondered why somebody doesn't do something about that. Then I realized I was somebody.
—*Lily Tomlin*

Don't worry that children never listen to you; worry that they are always watching you.
—*Robert Fulghum*

Success is to be measured not so much by the position that one has reached in life as by the obstacles which he has overcome.
—*Booker T. Washington*

Twenty years from now you will be more disappointed by the things you didn't do than by the ones you did do. So throw off the bowlines. Sail away from the safe harbor. Catch the trade winds in your sails. Explore. Dream. Discover.
—*Mark Twain*

Conflict lies at the core of innovation.
—*Emanuel R. Piore*

Don't be afraid of opposition. Remember, a kite rises against, not with, the wind.
—*Hamilton Mable*

The only difference between stumbling blocks and step-
ping stones is the way in which we use them.
—*Adriana Doyle*

The most intense conflicts, if overcome, leave behind a sense of security and
calm that is not easily disturbed. It is just these intense conflicts and their
conflagration which are needed to produce valuable and lasting results.
—*Carl G. Jung*

Sometimes you have to be silent to be heard.
—*Swiss proverb*

In one of our concert grand pianos, 243 taut strings exert a pull of 40,000 pounds
on an iron frame. It is proof that out of great tension may come great harmony.
—*Theodore E. Steinway*

To live unconsciously is to only live half a life.
—*Elizabeth Strout*

Afterword: Go Forth and Serve

The journey of a thousand miles begins with a single step.
—*Chinese proverb*

This book is only part of my journey in life. I'm hopeful that you found some inspiration and a few tools for your toolbox in these pages.

By simply picking up this book, you have expressed an interest in mentoring, in making a difference in the lives of others. By taking these stories to heart and finding your own heart, you have found the motivation to serve others simply by being there, by listening, and by inspiring.

The journey of life is hard, and the path is unknown, waiting to be discovered. Like most ventures, it is a richer venture when traveling with someone rather than going it alone.

Mentoring is a calling, a mission. In today's world there is a deep hunger for companionship, for reaching out, for a few kind words and a simple expression of "I care about you."

So care. Reach out. Extend a hand. Walk with someone. In taking that simple step, you will make a difference.

You will change the world.

Acknowledgments

This book came to life because of the hundreds of young men I've met and worked with over the last thirty-three years. They entered my life because of my work as a lawyer and judge and also as a stepfather, foster parent, and neighbor—and because they lived in the small town where I was born.

These boys who became men taught me about their hunger to be loved, their need for a place in this world, and their desire to grow into healthy, compassionate men—men who would feel at ease in their lives and in their roles as healthy men, husbands, and fathers, becoming good and productive members of the community. Their stories need to be heard.

I am also grateful for all the amazing people I have worked with and for the people who have supported me, reached out to me, and guided me along the way.

Judge Delbert Mayer; Michael Dooney; Jon Dwigans; John Wood; Maxine Hoggan; Ruth Smith; Jan Bartlett; Jean Lloyd; Madge Williams; Joan Imhoff; Dr. Don Balmer; Fr. Ray Ferguson, and my stepfather, Paul Miller, are only a few of the giants in my life whose wisdom and compassion have inspired me to write these words.

Kathy Van Loo, Jan Kent and Sandy Smith, great people I've worked with, have always told me to write a book. So I have.

I especially thank my editor at CreateSpace, Allan, and my readers and critics: Scott Allen, Karen Keltz, Wells Kempter, Sandra Pattin, and Alex Ramirez. And I thank Noe Martinez for his persistence and stubbornness to encourage me to finish this book.

About the Author

Neal C. Lemery is a retired judge and lawyer. He has served as the justice of the peace in Tillamook County, Oregon, where he was born; and he was also the municipal judge in five Oregon cities. He has also served as a pro tem circuit court judge in three counties and was the juvenile alternative court judge in his home county for many years. He has worked as a mediator and implemented a mediation program for small-claims cases.

He has also served as the elected district attorney and county counsel in Tillamook County, and he implemented a child-support collection program and criminal victims' assistance program there.

Mr. Lemery has also been active in various statewide organizations, serving as president of the Oregon Justices of the Peace Association and as a member of the Oregon Attorney General's sexual assault task force as well as president of the Oregon YMCAs. He has testified before the Oregon legislature and the Oregon Fish and Wildlife Commission on new legislation and regulations.

He is a former school board member and chair. The Northwest Oregon Educational Service District recognized him for his work on youth and educational issues. He has served on numerous community boards and task forces, and he is currently president of the Tillamook Bay Community College Foundation.

Mr. Lemery has written numerous op-ed articles for newspapers and has been published in *Mentor* magazine and the *North Coast Squid*, a literary review.

He is a native of Tillamook, Oregon, and is a fourth-generation Oregonian.

He currently mentors a number of young men incarcerated at the Tillamook campus of the Oregon Youth Authority, and he continues to encourage young people in his community to change their lives and achieve their dreams. In 2014 he was named the Oregon Youth Authority volunteer of the year in Tillamook County.

Mr. Lemery and his wife, Karen Keltz, a retired high school language and performing arts teacher, have been foster parents and have raised several boys, have led groups of high school students on trips to France, and continue to be advocates for youth and education. Karen Keltz is the author of *Sally Jo Survives Sixth Grade*, a middle-school novel that engages the reader to journal and focus on self-esteem and healthy relationships. She is writing another young-reader novel.

Mr. Lemery has a doctor of law (JD) degree from Willamette University College of Law in Salem, Oregon, and a BS degree in political science from Lewis and Clark College in Portland, Oregon. He has attended numerous workshops and classes on a variety of subjects, including sexual abuse and juvenile dependency issues; and has taught classes in law and other subjects, as he is a believer in lifelong education.

You can follow Mr. Lemery's adventures on his blog at http://www.neallemery.com or on Facebook at http://www.facebook.com/NealCLemery.

Made in the USA
Charleston, SC
05 February 2015